Accelerating Innovation

Management on the Cutting Edge series

Abbie Lundberg, series editor

Published in cooperation with *MIT Sloan Management Review*

Marco Bertini and Oded Koenigsberg, *The Ends Game: How Smart Companies Stop Selling Products and Start Delivering Value*

Christian Stadler, Julia Hautz, Kurt Matzler, and Stephan Friedrich von den Eichen, *Open Strategy: Mastering Disruption from Outside the C-Suite*

Gerald Kane, Rich Nanda, Anh Nguyen Phillips, and Jonathan Copulsky, *The Transformation Myth: Leading Your Organization through Uncertain Times*

Ron Adner, *Winning the Right Game: How to Disrupt, Defend, and Deliver in a Changing World*

Satish Nambisan and Yadong Luo, *The Digital Multinational: Navigating the New Normal in Global Business*

Ravin Jesuthasan and John W. Boudreau, *Work without Jobs: How to Reboot Your Organization's Work Operating System*

Mohan Subramaniam, *The Future of Competitive Strategy: Unleashing the Power of Data and Digital Ecosystems*

Chris B. Bingham and Rory M. McDonald, *Productive Tensions: How Every Leader Can Tackle Innovation's Toughest Trade-Offs*

Thomas H. Davenport and Steven M. Miller, *Working with AI: Real Stories of Human-Machine Collaboration*

Ravi Sarathy, *Enterprise Strategy for Blockchain: Lessons in Disruption from Fintech, Supply Chains, and Consumer Industries*

Lynda Gratton, *Redesigning Work: How to Transform Your Organization and Make Hybrid Work for Everyone*

John Horn, *Inside the Competitor's Mindset: How to Predict Their Next Move and Position Yourself for Success*

Elizabeth J. Altman, David Kiron, Jeff Schwartz, and Robin Jones, *Workforce Ecosystems: Reaching Strategic Goals with People, Partners, and Technologies*

Barbara H. Wixom, Cynthia M. Beath, and Leslie Owens, *Data Is Everybody's Business: The Fundamentals of Data Monetization*

Eric Siegel, *The AI Playbook: Mastering the Rare Art of Machine Learning Deployment*

Malia C. Lazu, *From Intention to Impact: A Practical Guide to Diversity, Equity, and Inclusion*

Daniel Aronson, *The Value of Values: How Leaders Can Grow Their Businesses and Enhance Their Careers by Doing the Right Thing*

Benjamin Laker, Lebene Soga, Yemisi Bolade-Ogunfodun, and Adeyinka Adewale, *Job Crafting*

Fred Selnes and Michael D. Johnson, *Customer Portfolio Management: Creating Value with a Large Leaky Bucket of Customers*

Phil Budden and Fiona Murray, *Accelerating Innovation: Competitive Advantage through Ecosystem Engagement*

MITSloan
Management Review

Accelerating Innovation

Competitive Advantage through Ecosystem Engagement

Phil Budden and Fiona Murray

The MIT Press
Cambridge, Massachusetts
London, England

The MIT Press
Massachusetts Institute of Technology
77 Massachusetts Avenue, Cambridge, MA 02139
mitpress.mit.edu

The MIT Press would like to thank the anonymous peer reviewers who provided comments on drafts of this book. The generous work of academic experts is essential for establishing the authority and quality of our publications. We acknowledge with gratitude the contributions of these otherwise uncredited readers.

This book was set in ITC Stone Serif Std and ITC Stone Sans Std by New Best-set Typesetters Ltd. Printed and bound in the United States of America.

Library of Congress Cataloging-in-Publication Data

Names: Budden, Phil, author. | Murray, Fiona E. S., author.
Title: Accelerating innovation : competitive advantage through ecosystem
    engagement / Phil Budden and Fiona Murray.
Description: Cambridge, Massachusetts : The MIT Press, [2025] | Series:
    Management on the cutting edge | Includes bibliographical references and index.
Identifiers: LCCN 2024032060 (print) | LCCN 2024032061 (ebook) |
    ISBN 9780262049610 (hardcover) | ISBN 9780262382182 (epub) |
    ISBN 9780262382199 (pdf)
Subjects: LCSH: Biotic communities. | Management.
Classification: LCC QH541 .B84 2025 (print) | LCC QH541 (ebook) |
    DDC 577.8/2—dc23/eng/20250113
LC record available at https://lccn.loc.gov/2024032060
LC ebook record available at https://lccn.loc.gov/2024032061

10 9 8 7 6 5 4 3 2 1

EU product safety and compliance information contact is: mitp-eu-gpsr@mit.edu

Contents

Series Foreword

The world does not lack for management ideas. Thousands of researchers, practitioners, and other experts produce tens of thousands of articles,
books, papers, posts, and podcasts each year. But only a scant few promise
to truly move the needle on practice, and fewer still dare to reach into
the future of what management will become. It is this rare breed of idea—
meaningful to practice, grounded in evidence, and *built for the future*—that
we seek to present in this series.

Abbie Lundberg

Editor in chief
MIT Sloan Management Review

Introduction

Leaders in large organizations face continuous pressure to innovate. But no company, government agency, or nonprofit has all the resources, time, or talent it needs to keep up with the rapid advances in innovation and in science and technology (S&T). Their leaders know they should look beyond their own organizations to support their internal innovation efforts, but the external landscape can seem bewildering.

Globally, there are:

- over 100,000 scientific papers published each week;
- more than 3 million patents filed every year; and
- thousands of venture capital (VC) deals: in 2022 alone, investors funded over 15,000 entrepreneurs in the United States and 35,000 worldwide.

Luckily, this vast and changing innovation landscape is navigable, if you have a good map to guide you. Researchers, entrepreneurs, and investors congregate in geographic hotspots—where they tend to specialize. We call these *innovation ecosystems*.* In the United States, they include the iconic Silicon Valley and Greater Boston, which are well-known for web-based digital technology and biotechnology, respectively. There is much already written about those two places, but this innovation ecosystem logic is not

---

*Books about innovation are full of buzzwords: while we've written this handbook so it's as buzzword-light as possible, there are some terms that you will want to know about. In this (our one!) footnote, we wish to inform you that, whenever we use a term that deserves demystifying, we put it in italics, like *innovation ecosystems*. If you want to know more about a term beyond what is in the body of the book, you can refer to our glossary at https://corporateinnovation.mit.edu, or see under "Resources" on this book's page at the MIT Press website.

a purely American (or even Western) phenomenon. There are other innovation ecosystems around the world, with varieties of entrepreneurship
just like there are *varieties of capitalism*, covering a wider range of sectors,
so we will purposefully try to take you to new locations, with more varied sectors.[1] These include Singapore (smart cities), Perth (mining), Cairo
and Dubai (*fintech*); London and Lagos (fintech and media), Copenhagen
(*quantum computing*), Rio de Janeiro (energy), Halifax (oceans), and Tel Aviv
(cybersecurity). We will return to these places throughout the book to draw
out insights about how to effectively engage with an ecosystem (wherever
you are in the world) to support your organization's innovation goals. This
will also demonstrate that this innovation ecosystem logic is truly a global
phenomenon.

Over the past decade, we have helped hundreds of corporate and government leaders to become more efficient and effective at working with
innovators outside their organizations to complement their internal efforts
at innovation. Rather than spreading themselves thinly around the globe,
they have learned to focus their efforts and work closely with entrepreneurs, find the specialist resources they need from universities, and team
up with *risk capital* providers in a handful of ecosystems—and then experiment rapidly to get the results they need and meet the goals they have set
for themselves.

We wrote this book as a practical guide to accelerating your innovation
through ecosystem engagement. While this engagement is not enough (as
impact ultimately depends on a successful series of later steps, as well as
clarity up front about what you want to accomplish), it can go wrong if you
don't start out right. Though informed by extensive research and reading
across the separate fields of tech, innovation, entrepreneurship, and strategic management, we have tried to distill insights and interconnections
from all these different worlds into a useful and globally applicable set of
frameworks and models.

What Leaders Get Wrong about External Innovation

When organizations venture into an ecosystem in search of innovation,
they often fail to get the results they seek. In our work with teams, in our
MIT classrooms, as consultants, and as researchers, we have diagnosed
some of the key reasons why they fall short.

Typically, it's because they have neglected to ask themselves three critical questions:

- *What* do they need from innovation?
- *Who* should they engage externally?
- *How* can they best achieve their goals?

We find that leaders often have unrealistic expectations of the results they can gain because they rushed (with enthusiasm!) into relationships and projects without strategically thinking about what they are trying to accomplish, identifying who can best help them—plus why anyone in an ecosystem would bother—and planning how to proceed.

Beyond answering these three questions, we find that many organizations then lack concrete plans and clear processes to integrate the innovations they develop with external partners back into their innovation systems, that is, *pull-through*. This requires leaders who will encourage and support their teams in diagnosing and overcoming political and cultural barriers to ideas from outside. The "not invented here" syndrome sadly persists as a mindset in many organizations and is a challenge for innovation leaders, even when they are also focused on external innovations and the allure of ideas generated outside their organizations.

To illustrate how some leaders are effectively navigating these challenges, we'll look at two examples. First, we have Mike Fanning, the longtime CEO of MassMutual. The company, founded in 1851, provides insurance and retirement products to five million hardworking customers. Mike was the visionary behind the gleaming seventeenth-floor glass high-rise in Boston's Seaport District that serves as the organization's headquarters and innovation space. Before we connected with him in 2018, Mike and his team had relocated key members of his innovation group there from the gray headquarters buildings of Springfield in Central Massachusetts.

The team's new neighborhood, situated on Boston's Atlantic-facing seaport at the eastern end of the humming I-90 interstate, was dubbed an "innovation district" by the mayor of Boston at the time. Mike and his leadership team believed it would be easy to attract early-stage *start-up* entrepreneurs with an interest in financial services—a sector these impatient entrepreneurs, who congregated there, refer to as *fintech*—to help update the firm's insurance and retirement businesses with new digital products.

As the plan unfolded, it became clear that this would not be as easy as opening a new front door. The entrepreneurs in the Seaport District saw MassMutual as too traditional, and they were not sure what the company wanted from them anyway. The team Mike had sent mainly connected with start-ups whose growth paths were too slow to make a difference to MassMutual or whose need for corporate partnerships was not really clear. Many start-ups were hoping to disrupt the financial sector, not partner with it, and so they were poor matches for the large, established insurer.

Only when Mike began to work closely with MassChallenge (MC), a large local *accelerator* working with hundreds of early-stage start-ups each year, did MassMutual make progress. The MC accelerator team helped Mass-Mutual identify entrepreneurs with the ideas they needed and gave them a community where they could connect. Equally important, MassMutual started to reshape its internal innovation system to align its priorities, people, and processes with the ecosystem. This included staffing its innovation teams with younger, more entrepreneurially minded employees. As part of cementing their role within MC, MassMutual provided space in their new building for the entire MC team and its many start-up ventures, while also contributing mentoring and expertise for the accelerator's cohorts of entrepreneurs.

For the second example, we have Belinda (as we'll call her), a senior leader in a European government agency. Her team focused on service delivery, ensuring the agency's frontline employees had access to the same sorts of leading-edge innovations as private sector employees working in similarly fast-paced and high-stress departments.

Belinda's team scouted their country for solutions, attending numerous accelerator *demo-days* and *pitch* sessions. However, they became frustrated by the low yield from their efforts. To make matters worse, every time they brought in a new technology, the agency's processes for integrating it into operations stalled their efforts. Procurement *acquisition* was slow and risk averse, the rules around intellectual property (IP) imposed by the government on start-ups were frustrating, and it seemed that the two parties simply could not find a way to connect. The team, as well as Belinda's boss, became increasingly frustrated that they could never scale any solutions that solved problems for a handful of employees in a way that would make a difference to the agency as a whole. Likewise, an attempt to build an internal VC unit to fund relevant start-up ventures was deemed by government ministers as too costly, potentially risky, and too untethered from the agency's mission.

When we met Belinda in 2016, she was about to give up. Instead, we suggested that her team identify a small number of internal problem owners who would benefit from service delivery innovation and involve them in the search for the right ecosystems and the right external teams. We advised them to focus on a few places and work only with those handful of accelerators and investors that aligned best with the problems they wanted to solve. The team discovered that there were indeed a few hotspots around the country with the relevant expertise. Additionally, each community of innovators, though small, included entrepreneurs interested in meaningful engagement to solve some of the agency's hardest challenges.

Rather than provide many pathways to interact, we also suggested that Belinda and her team choose a few types of collaboration, including some simple investment approaches, competitions, and some streamlined contracts. The team still had to adapt the internal system so that it could adopt external ideas, but the focus on fewer ecosystems and on better ways to interact quickly led to stronger interactions and a deeper understanding between the internal and external teams.

A Handbook for Ecosystem Engagement

This book will tell you how to work successfully within innovation ecosystems, just as Mike at MassMutual and Belinda, the government agency executive, learned to do. If you are a leader in a large public, nonprofit, or private sector organization, and if you have a stake in how it innovates—and, like us, you are convinced that innovation ecosystems are essential to your strategic goals—then we can help you get the most from your interactions with ecosystem stakeholders, including entrepreneurs, researchers, and investors.

Our approach is based on what we have learned from leaders in sectors as diverse as mining, banking, healthcare, infrastructure, security, and defense, as well as studying more than sixty innovation ecosystems on six continents. We have tested our ideas with corporate leaders and government change agents, students in our executive programs, and with many academic colleagues at MIT and in universities around the world who are interested in innovation ecosystems and want to improve their own.

We will show you the logic behind the strategies of large organizations, including perhaps some surprising ones (in sectors such as aerospace, mining, energy, and defense) that are emerging as some of the most effective at innovation. Companies in these sectors, like others we'll showcase, have moved their talented teams closer to hubs of innovation ecosystem activity. They have curated portfolios of external engagements with start-ups, university research centers, and government labs, often working in close collaboration with risk capital providers (especially venture funds) as well as with accelerators, hackathons, and independent innovation studios. And they have created internal structures and processes through which they can reap the rewards of their investments of time, attention, and resources.

Not only have they led these efforts from the top, but they have also empowered their employees to go out into the ecosystem to learn and connect with other stakeholders. And they have recognized and addressed the role of culture in overcoming the frictions that arise when you turn your innovation efforts outward.

Like these companies, you will learn how to transform your external innovation efforts from a well-intentioned but messy, and often bewildering, set of projects and relationships, into a high-value, streamlined, and strategic program of activities.

To give you a sense of how the book is structured, we will now briefly set out the direction of travel, chapter by chapter, as follows:

Chapter 1, "Innovation, Ecosystems, and Their Stakeholders," defines what we mean by place-based innovation ecosystems (as opposed to corporate ecosystems). We introduce the five key stakeholders of the MIT model, especially the entrepreneurs and their start-up ventures, which are so effective at innovation (as we will describe it). We then set out why these innovation ecosystems matter to large organizations and what they might offer to you—specifically as sources of novel ideas, with access to specialized resources, and ways of experimenting that reduce risk.

Chapter 2, "What You Need from an Innovation Ecosystem," digs into working out "what" you need, based on what you are doing already, and how best to fill those gaps. This systematic approach helps leaders avoid leaping ahead to specific initiatives—that is, the "how" of ecosystem engagement—before they are clear about what they need, and the specific types of ecosystem stakeholders—that is, the "who"—that can help them with that.

Chapter 3, "Who to Engage in an Ecosystem," looks more closely at the three key stakeholders at the apex of the MIT model, namely entrepreneurs, universities, and risk capital providers. Within the category of entrepreneurs, we encourage you to look for the subset of start-ups that are likely to become the most impactful. The right university or risk capital stakeholder can help find these elusive entrepreneurs.

Chapter 4, "How to Engage in an Ecosystem," introduces a model of the many programs and practices out in the wild of external ecosystem. Broken into clear cycles, this framework will help you better target the "what" and the "who" identified in the prior chapters. Many large organizations have copied these ecosystem cycles for internal use, often calling them *stages* in an internal *pipeline*. The chapter will explore why the ecosystem can be more effective at this Darwinian process but also how large organizations can benefit from these practices in the wild.

Chapter 5, "Leadership for Ecosystem Engagement," provides a three-level model for distributed leadership that is needed for organizations generally but especially those seeking innovation from ecosystem engagement.[2] Each level of leader reading this book will have important but different roles to play on the "what, who and how" questions. A key task is selecting the right leaders for the right role, especially for engaging the other stakeholders, and then navigating the pull-through of external innovation into and through the internal pipeline.

Chapter 6, "Political and Cultural Challenges," explains how to address these when working in ecosystems. We build on chapter 5 by explaining how innovation leaders get results from their investment into the ecosystem of internal resources, time, and talent. We show how top leaders set strategic direction for ecosystem interactions and optimize their internal system from the top, how frontline leaders engage ecosystem stakeholders, and how middle managers help integrate the results from the ecosystem interactions back into the organization, all while accounting for some of the hardest cultural and political challenges that lead to failure, however well-intentioned the plan.

Chapter 7, "'Doing Good' While Also 'Doing Well,'" sets out how large organizations (both public and private) can do well by extracting innovation advantage from ecosystem engagement while contributing positively to the wider ecosystem and other stakeholders. Not only can large organizations shape ecosystems as a long-term source of strategic benefit to themselves, but they can also help place-based ecosystems—nested in wider communities—evolve in ways that meet social and economic goals.

In the appendix, we offer some brief advice, shifting readers toward a plan for action that will help them make progress with innovation.

Turning now to chapter 1, we will first look more closely at what we mean by innovation ecosystems and their stakeholders, and ask "what is innovation anyway?"

1 Innovation, Ecosystems, and Their Stakeholders

Eighteenth-century London was an unlikely place for innovation and innovators to flourish. And yet it was one of the most innovative places during one of the most innovative periods in history. The precursor elements of what became the Industrial Revolution had begun there, under gray skies, despite poor sewage systems and decades of political unrest (including two political revolutions in the prior century).

In explaining this seemingly odd fact, economic historians have recognized that the density of innovators with exciting ideas made London special at that time.[1] Combined with key foundational institutions, such as rule of law and monetary stability, these innovators found fertile ground for taking forward their ideas entrepreneurially. Collectively, these allowed for the emergence of specialized resources—commercial financing of risky projects, scientific societies, and newly wealthy customers—which supported the ambitions of entrepreneurs who sought to test their novel ideas.

With a physical proximity that must have at times felt stifling (not to mention dangerous), Londoners from different social classes, religions, and experiences who had distinct ambitions came together and exchanged ideas and resources. Among their favorite places to meet were bustling coffee houses—like the first one, near the Royal Exchange, opened by Pasque Rosée—where the main substance on offer (coffee, of course) promised greater alertness than the beer in the traditional English pub. There, scientists, inventors, and investors mingled with intellectuals, poets, politicians, and entrepreneurs.

In London, inventors found the resources they needed to finance and build new ventures that would eventually scale the globe. These resources also supported the rest of the country to build their new ventures and finance their steam engines, navigational clocks, spinning machines, and iron furnaces. Moreover, ambitious individuals found a culture and community that encouraged their experimentation, allowing for learning and adaptation within the confines of the city and out into the regions where many of their growing markets could be found.

Talent attracts talent, investment attracts investment, and experimenting leads to learning and ultimately economic growth. The same dynamic that fueled innovation in eighteenth-century London is robust today. For example, a recent study of US patents (a simple proxy for the invention phase of innovation) found that GDP per worker (a productivity measure) was $16,000 higher in areas of the country where the number of inventions were concentrated.[2] Not surprisingly, government leaders around the world have recently sought to turn their cities and regions into the next Silicon "X" (e.g., glen or wadi) or "Y" (e.g., AI (*artificial intelligence*) Valley.[3]

A good starting point for leaders in large organizations who wish to tap into the potential of innovation ecosystems is to understand what they are, to know their key stakeholders, and to recognize how ecosystems drive and support innovation. These are foundations upon which we will build throughout the rest of the book.

What Is Innovation, Anyway?

Before we go on, it's important to establish a working definition of what *innovation* is and, more importantly, what it means in your context. We will share with you MIT's working definition, not because anyone has a monopoly on wisdom but because its approach informs our work and helps us make our case for the rest of the book. It may also help you to communicate clearly across your organization when you apply our advice.

Our practical definition (from MIT's Innovation Initiative [MITii]) is simple:

> Innovation is the "process of taking ideas from inception to impact."[4]

Some people associate the concept of innovation with novelty and invention (and we have elsewhere described innovation ecosystems as cauldrons of novel and inventive ideas). For others, it evokes an end result: the transformation of a business or industry (certainly the goal of many entrepreneurs as well as established businesses) or perhaps the accomplishment of a mission (often the goal of a government department or agency). But our approach emphasizes what happens between these points. For MIT, one key aspect is that the definition does not include the word technology, even though we are famously an institute of technology. This is not because technology is not important (it clearly is, and is more than just tech, by which many mean digital software) but rather because innovation is a much larger phenomenon.

At the heart of our definition is the concept of the "idea," which we regard as a hypothetical match between a problem and a solution. The better the proposed match between the problem and the solution, the better the idea. More than simply a moment of invention, innovation in our "process" definition implies taking deliberate steps from that initial idea in a chosen direction rather than a "random walk." Innovation's starting point might be either a moment of inspiration or a structured process of idea generation (i.e., *ideation*), but it has a destination and milestones along the way.

Simply having an idea is not enough to count as innovation: it also needs to result in "impact." It is for you and your organization to decide on the destination and thus the impact you wish to have: for a particular group of customers or end users; to meet a goal for profitability, efficiency, or sustainability; or a wider aim such as improved national security, greater climate resilience, or healthier communities. With an eye on the desired impact, innovative teams work backward from that to the starting point— an idea or hypothesis that could, in some way, meet that particular goal.

As a process, innovation takes resources to progress through all the phases necessary to develop it fully. At every phase, teams will require different sorts of people with different skills, experiences, and perspectives. Moreover, the resources that support the beginning of the journey will be different from those needed closer to the end, when companies are scaling delivery of a product or service and achieving global impact. For example, the sorts of financing needed at the start of the innovation process will be different from those needed as ideas are scaled: not only will the amounts differ but also the risk appetite, leading to different types of financing approaches by phase. Similarly, the physical resources and materials will change as innovations move from an idea in someone's head, to a sketch or a model, and to a full-scale, completed product.

Marshaling the right resources is a key leadership responsibility. So is designing a process that describes how ideas will be identified, sets expectations for learning and experimentation, and includes waypoints (often known as milestones) to evaluate whether to stop or continue development (because many ideas will not, and should not, survive to the end). The process does not need to be rigid: it could be messy and creative. But it should reflect your organization's priorities. And as we have emphasized in our introduction, our focus in writing this book is to guide you as you take advantage of external innovation ecosystems to support some of your organization's highest innovation priorities and especially at the early stage of your innovation journeys. With that, it is useful to turn to what we mean when we say innovation ecosystem.

What Is an Innovation Ecosystem?

Most of us can name at least a few hotspots of innovation around the globe: Silicon Valley and Boston, of course, but also London and Munich, Rio de Janeiro and Cairo, Singapore and Tel Aviv, among others. As the power and potential of these vibrant places have permeated the public consciousness, they have become known by different labels—clusters, hubs, districts, precincts. We call them *innovation ecosystems* because, like natural ecosystems, they feature diverse but interacting actors (like species in the natural world), each with an essential role in enabling the environment to thrive and evolve and, importantly, each with a greater or lesser interdependency upon the others.

In our decade of studying more than sixty innovation ecosystems across six continents, including our local one (i.e., Greater Boston), we have identified several attributes of these unique locations:

- They typically have an urban core, with populations in the millions, but are often not defined by traditional political boundaries.
- They usually include research-intensive universities, especially ones designed to translate that research into impact.
- They support a high concentration of innovative activity, especially at the early, even precommercial, stages of the innovation journey.

Innovation ecosystems are full of researchers, inventors, start-up founders, and other stakeholders who seek new ways to solve problems and who rely on one another for their success. But they are more than just places where people with ideas congregate. Ecosystems also concentrate the specialized resources that are needed to support them: expertise in prototyping, equipment for testing products, experience in developing production methods, investors who understand risk-taking early-stage ventures, customers willing to try new solutions, and even government policies that support new-to-the-world activities rather than stifle them.

Some innovators must work in proximity with one another because they require and benefit from shared physical infrastructure such as wet labs, maker spaces, and machine shops. Communications technologies allow others to operate in greater isolation or more remotely from these dense ecosystems. However, research shows that location matters regardless of what sorts of innovations you are working on.[5] Innovators cluster together—again, especially in those early stages—because they benefit from being close to other talented people, nearby to investors who understand the risks they take, and in easy distance to other, more experienced entrepreneurs. The opportunity for in-person interaction is enough to drive them to these hotspots for the start of their innovation journey, even when the costs of living and working in these places are higher than in more suburban or even semirural locations.

Beyond simply being close to a wide range of useful individuals and specialized resources, we also find that proximity is the basis for building a sustainable community. People share expertise, exchange resources, learn rapidly, and try again when something fails. This sharing means that they are interdependent. And with this dependency comes density as innovators and their stakeholders create a culture of exchange and learning that continuously supports and accelerates the innovation process from an initial idea to the later stages of impact, for example, commercialization and global scaling when individuals, teams, and ventures branch out around the country and the world.

Finally, innovation ecosystems are distinct from *corporate ecosystems*, which are anchored by an established business or industry. Typical corporate ecosystems are more widely dispersed across the globe and structured around commercial relationships, such as supply chains and contracts, and so are often also called value chains. These corporate ecosystems can play a role in innovation, too, but usually to the primary advantage of the incumbent anchor, and they are more usually focused on the later stages of innovation, such as growth. They may support start-ups in later stages of innovation by helping them to reduce costs, drive efficiency, and expand their reach to a wide range of customers, but corporate ecosystems typically support innovators only across their specific platform or their supply chains.

A large organization can benefit from both types of ecosystems. Consider Google. This trillion-dollar web company (now a unit of Alphabet) famously anchors a corporate ecosystem around its headquarters in Mountain View, California, in the heart of Silicon Valley. From there, it extends its reach across the globe through its other corporate locations and its eponymous search engine into homes and offices worldwide. It also has a "value chain" that comprises a series of contracting partners, independent app developers, and many digital advertisers who build and use both its digital platform and the suite of highly interconnected digital tools and services that shape the consumer and workplace experience.

Despite being web focused, Google also benefits from the sorts of location-specific innovation ecosystems that we are interested in. When the company was looking to move into mobile telecoms and couldn't find the solutions it needed to complement its Silicon Valley web software (either inside the company or around Silicon Valley), it found and ultimately acquired Android: a small team of scrappy entrepreneurs in the Cambridge Innovation Center building, which overlooks the MIT campus. The rather ugly, concrete high-rise near the Kendall Square subway stop was built in 1969 and once hosted MIT-spinout Raytheon—a defense contractor that specializes in cutting-edge electronics and guidance systems. (In 2020, Raytheon merged with United Technologies to form RTX.)

Android isn't the only start-up that Google has drawn into its corporate system from its deep engagement with innovation ecosystems somewhere else in the world and scaled for millions of customers. When the company sought a way to monetize search to pay for its apparently free web services, it turned to New York and its advertising cluster. There, Google found an *adtech* start-up venture called DoubleClick that it seamlessly integrated into its search engine to allow it to more accurately target web advertising. For cyber-enabled geolocation (across cellphones), Google turned to Tel Aviv for a start-up venture called Waze, which it scaled across all of its platforms and made its Maps more accurate. And more recently, Google bought DeepMind for its AI strengths in *deep learning* (DL), after years of engagement with the London ecosystem through its Google campus and other activities. The acquisition has been a source of talent, ideas, and solutions for Google's AI activities, including speech-to-text, and the energy efficiency of their data centers, among others (and has now been integrated to create Google DeepMind).

Google has chosen to open innovation-focused units to connect with start-ups in technology hotspots including Seoul, Sao Paolo, Tokyo, and Warsaw, where it taps into creative talent and emerging ideas. And it has innovation hubs in cities from London to Lagos to the United Arab Emirates. If even the most web-based company out of Silicon Valley finds benefit in an innovation ecosystem strategy, then it is worth studying this phenomenon further.

The Key Stakeholders in Innovation Ecosystems

Now that we have established what makes innovation ecosystems special places, we can look deeper to see who is there.

The multistakeholder model developed at MIT defines five key stakeholders found together in the most effective innovation ecosystems: entrepreneurs, universities, risk capital providers, corporations, and the government. Of course, such places in the world include a whole variety of other players (such as citizens, customers, nongovernmental organizations). However, these stakeholders are the "minimum viable players" (another use of the *MVP* acronym) needed in an innovation ecosystem to support the research, translation, experimentation, and commercialization that are essential to both scientific and technological discovery, and the application of these discoveries to important challenges and opportunities (see figure 1.1).

Though you can find these stakeholders individually wherever you look around the world—in the communities, organizations, markets, and industries that make up the global economy—when they come together with critical mass and with a high degree of interconnectivity and interdependency (sometimes literally "around the same table"), they can propel the dynamism of their innovation ecosystem through supporting the earliest, most risky stages of the innovation process.

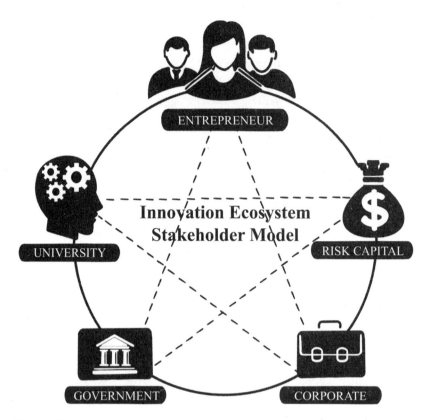

Figure 1.1
MIT's five-stakeholder model.
Source: Phil Budden and Fiona Murray, "MIT's Stakeholder Framework for Building and Accelerating Innovation Ecosystems" (working paper, MIT REAP, 2024), p. 8, https://reap.mit.edu/assets/MIT-Stakeholder-Framework_Innovation-Ecosystems-23 .pdf.

Our model of five stakeholders expands the set of stakeholders from those who were regarded as the drivers of innovation in the twentieth century. Research into that era highlighted the role of government and corporations in forming public/private partnerships. By midcentury, scholars added universities to the mix and, with a later nod to the emerging field of genetics, dubbed the three players the *Triple Helix*.[6] The Manhattan Project, as captured in the 2023 film *Oppenheimer*, illustrates how the Triple Helix functioned. During World War II, the US government financed faculty from leading universities and experts from a small number of companies to build a system (a national laboratory in Los Alamos, New Mexico) that would deliver tremendous novelty (the atom bomb) at great speed, under conditions of extreme uncertainty.

The same model of government, university, and industry cooperation served as the foundation of the US space program, and it spurred US vaccine development in the 1940s. In the United Kingdom, the development of penicillin followed a similar model, and in Taiwan, the storied semiconductor industry emerged through cooperation among the government, industry, and universities. Toward the end of the century, however, these three stakeholders no longer had a monopoly on innovation. At times, they were slow to seek out new ideas, constrained by their existing resources and organizational design. For some, limited competition and near monopolies meant they were less open to experimentation. Their contributions to innovation were no longer sufficient.

Enter—or reenter—the entrepreneurs and risk capital providers (think back to London and the first Industrial Revolution). During the past forty years, these players have become more essential, working in cooperation, or at times in competition, with large corporations but still interacting with the government and universities.

Examples of the increasing role of entrepreneurs and risk capital abound. In the life sciences, the shift toward start-up entrepreneurs and risk capital providers working closely with universities was pioneered in San Francisco and Greater Boston with the founding of ventures such as Genentech, Biogen, and Genzyme. In place of the National Aeronautics and Space Administration (NASA) and a handful of defense corporations in the space program, we now have the entrepreneurial start-up SpaceX and its investors. And more recently, the same collection of stakeholders has formed new relationships in support of next-generation climate solutions in batteries, industrial processes, and carbon capture in Greater Boston and especially in the European ecosystems of Stockholm and Zurich. In cities like New York, Berlin, Cairo, and Lagos, digital technology and especially fintech have strongly emerged with a similar set of stakeholders.

Another military example really clarifies how dramatically the innovation landscape has evolved. The response to the war in Ukraine has involved not only governments and traditional defense corporations but also, to a lesser extent, universities. Moreover, a figurative army of entrepreneurs and investors supports innovation on the front line. Start-ups, such as Hacken and UnderDefense, for example, are providing cybersecurity technology. Established and new risk capital providers such as D3, Ukrainian Tech Ventures, and SID Venture Partners have financed a range of innovations to support the war effort, address humanitarian challenges, and bolster the wider economy. This has fueled a burgeoning innovation ecosystem in Ukraine and across the border in Poland, with VCs investing over $800 million in the region since 2021.

The shift to a five-stakeholder model means that innovation leaders in government, large corporations, and nonprofits can no longer rely on their internal innovation systems or a few partnerships to tap into the frontiers of innovation. And this trend seems here to stay on account of the enduring nature of the wide array of factors in the global economy that have influenced these changes.

First is the fact that small, focused entrepreneurial teams are highly effective at pursuing novel and risky ideas to address important problems and challenges. We see this in ventures like Boston Metal and Sublime Systems in Greater Boston, which are developing greener steel and cement, respectively. In Cairo, the start-up Fawry is creating new digital solutions for banking, and Veezeta is doing the same for healthcare.[7] In Stockholm, VoltaTrucks is providing electric trucking as a service, while NorthVolt raised over a billion dollars to expand its production of novel batteries.

Second, investors are increasingly willing to fund entrepreneurs who are working on ideas at the frontier of science such as fusion energy or quantum computing, provided that the potential "risk/reward" payoff from finding a scalable solution to a large and important problem is big enough. Indeed, the data suggests a growing allocation of almost 20 percent of VC into what is often known as *deep tech*, that is, businesses based on transformative S&T, innovating in fields like life sciences, new materials, semiconductors, and future telecoms. Financial capital has crowded into such companies from specialized investors supported by large pension funds, endowments, and sovereign wealth funds, amplifying the influence of both private investors and the entrepreneurs they support.

These start-ups and their investors are highly concentrated in innovation ecosystems due to the specialized talent and infrastructure that they require, and are more easily accessed and shared when they are colocated. By building new ventures in close proximity to one another and adjacent to specialized infrastructure, the risks and challenges can be balanced and shared. It is only when these ventures grow beyond their most fragile founding stages to scaling and expansion that the ecosystem logic may hold less, and they escape well beyond the confines of a particular geography, bringing jobs and wealth to a wider range of regions.

Third, the changing dynamics among start-ups and risk capital providers are matched by shifts in the culture of academia (at least in some parts of it). University faculty and students in the physical and life sciences (as well as computer science), and across many branches of engineering, have found that an exciting and effective way to get their ideas out of the lab and into the world is now through start-ups. Today, many young innovators have chosen careers in start-up ventures that are better at risk-taking and experiment-running, rather than in large, stable organizations.

Indeed, we have found that over the last several decades, students are increasingly focusing their careers on entrepreneurship as a way to have impact. A survey of MIT alumni found that over a third now become entrepreneurs, and over the past thirty years of graduates, the average age at which they start their companies has been getting steadily younger.[8] This trend is matched in studies from Stanford University graduates. While these numbers are much higher than the population at large, all age groups in the US have experienced an increase in the rate of first-time entrepreneurship.

Likewise, a growing number of university faculty are submitting patents and pursuing start-ups based on this IP (often with their students), not simply writing academic papers: over 4 percent of US patents are filed by universities.[9] Many leading technical universities and research labs around the world now serve as the anchors of innovation ecosystems by generating novel ideas at a significant rate.[10] They range from MIT and Harvard in Greater Boston to the Technical University of Munich (TUM) in Germany or ETH Zurich (known in English as the Federal Institute of Technology) in Switzerland.

Why Do Innovation Ecosystems Matter to Large Organizations?

At every phase along the innovation journey, you have an opportunity to link your internal innovation system to an external innovation ecosystem. If you are a leader of a large organization intent on delivering a robust innovation strategy, you are unlikely to find all the talent and resources you need just within your organization. Innovation ecosystems and their stakeholders can support your goals and priorities at each stage but especially at the start. As such, they can be a source of competitive advantage.

The experience of Pieter Wolters, an innovation leader at DSM Venturing, is a case in point.[11] The organization, which today focuses on health and nutrition for humans, animals, and the planet, has a storied history of internal research and development (R&D). It synthesized the first vitamin supplements in the 1930s, and more recently, it developed feed additives to reduce cow methane emissions.

But Pieter's team was finding it hard to discover solutions to some of the challenges of climate and sustainability that DSM Venturing identified as large potential market opportunities. The young, talented material scientists and chemists with ideas in these areas were more inclined to join startups. Even when Pieter did find an idea internally, he struggled to allocate the right resources. Perhaps most importantly, the internal system moved slowly, committed to a rigid, *stage-gate* process, with a six-month review cycle. It was not designed for exploring new markets and customers with rapidly changing needs.

Many leaders in large organizations are similarly limited in their ability to deliver on their innovation strategy. Their internal system is not always a source for the best, most diverse ideas and people. Government leaders like Belinda (whom we met in the introduction) can find it especially challenging to attract the right personnel. Young innovators may not wish to commit to the lower pay of the civil service or adapt to what they imagine is a rigid bureaucracy.

The leaders we have talked to also know that their organizations cannot always be optimized to provide the specialized resources that it takes to nurture these ideas in their earliest stages—whether it is access to particular customers, certain types of financing, or specialized testbeds. This was the situation for Mike, the MassMutual CEO (also from the introduction), who found it was impossible to adequately test some of the newer ideas in finance and insurance technology due to the company's size and scale. Insurance is also subject to strict regulation, and the leadership team felt the weight of the reputational responsibilities of being a large and storied organization, worried about the risks of public failure that might accompany testing and experimentation.

Further, as Pieter experienced, large organizations have often solidified around slow, bureaucratic processes that deliver *business as usual* (BAU) but stifle the ability to experiment, cycle through alternatives, learn quickly, and move on. This process, however, is essential to the early stages of the innovation journey, before the relentless efficiency of mission impact or customer delivery sets in. Belinda also found this a challenge, not least because of how annual government funding was tied to executing projects rather than achieving outcomes.

Luckily for Pieter, Belinda, Mike, and many ambitious leaders, we see no reason for them to be trapped by their internal systems. Innovation ecosystems across the globe can provide three benefits that are not only valuable but also hard to generate solely from inside—novel ideas, specialized resources, and experimentation—which we now list briefly, before considering each in turn at greater length.

First, more than other locations, innovation ecosystems are characterized by a dense concentration of novel and exciting ideas. The range of new thinking and new ideas is hard for any one organization to emulate internally, making ecosystems an alternative source of insights that could provide the starting points for innovators tackling critical organizational priorities.

The second benefit of ecosystems is the density of specialized resources that support the innovation journey, especially those essential to the early stages of *ideation*, concept development, prototyping, and piloting. Ecosystems have the technical expertise, dedicated risk capital, and tailored infrastructure that may be distinct from the resources a large organization can easily access. The density and diversity of resources from ecosystems can accelerate the innovation process within large organizations by eliminating the need to build expertise or infrastructure in-house.

And third, we have found that ecosystems support risk-taking and risk reduction through *experimentation*. Experimentation is often the hardest practice to emulate in large organizations, which tend to have low tolerance for uncertainty or failure.

Let's look at each of these benefits in more detail.

A Source for Novel Ideas

Innovation ecosystems are replete with ideas. In our definition, an idea, especially at the start, is simply a rough-and-ready match between a problem and a solution—to be improved upon or abandoned. When we consider an idea to be a "problem/solution match," it helps us widen our perspective and explore many, sometimes unusual or untested, types of solutions.

Likewise, our definition allows us to understand problems more broadly than simply a set of specifications, but rather as a problem to solve or a challenge to be overcome.

Take, for example, the problem of the climate impact of construction. Framed as a problem (rather than a market), one solution might be to change building methods to reduce the use of cement. But other approaches might be to remove the CO_2 from cement with new chemistry—as Boston-based Sublime Systems and Poland's CemVision are doing—or instead to make an entirely new biological cement, like Colorado-based Prometheus Materials, that could serve as a substitute.[12]

We can assess solutions and problems according to their degree of novelty. *BAU* is where today's problems and solutions are already matched. Beyond that, low-novelty solutions and problems tend to be well understood. The problems are similar to others previously encountered; solutions offer incremental improvements and developing them carries relatively little risk. Higher-novelty solutions and problems—often out at the furthest *horizon*—can test the limits of our knowledge. The problems are new to us, and the solutions push the boundaries of scientific inquiry, making them complex and risky.

To visualize the variety of problem/solution matches—and how they might align with what an innovation ecosystem has to offer—we plot them on a matrix (figure 1.2).

On the horizontal (x) axis, we plot the degree of solution-novelty (and risk) out to the far horizon. On the vertical (y) axis, it's the degree of problem-novelty (and risk) that goes out to that horizon. From this, we can identify a series of innovation horizons.[13] Each horizon focuses on increasing novelty and, consequently, is accompanied by higher risks of delivering the proposed idea for your organization (and as such a higher chance of innovation projects failing to meet desired goals).

As we look out toward the furthest horizon—a very relevant area for ecosystem engagement—we find what we call *Big I* innovation efforts. Think of these as aiming for *10x* impact (similar to how start-up founders and their VC funders often seek 10x scaling of their product, or 10x returns on their investment). Sometimes projects in this part of the innovation matrix are referred to as *moonshots* (named after the US Apollo 11 spaceflight program from the 1960s). Out at the furthest edges of problem/solution matches, some of the most radical innovations may even fall beyond the

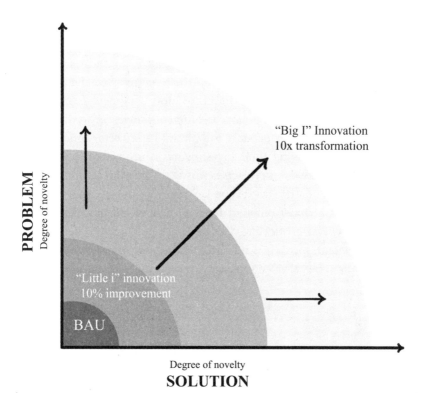

Figure 1.2
Innovation from BAU, toward higher-novelty problems and solutions.

furthest horizon (as visible to you) into what is effectively the *whitespace* of innovation.

At the other end of the innovation spectrum (but less relevant to innovation ecosystem engagement) is an important zone, closer to BAU, which is what we call *little i* innovation. These projects are more than just business improvement or incremental advancements to operational excellence, such as through the *Toyota Way* of lean manufacturing, *kaizen*, and *Six Sigma*.[14] These *little i* innovations, with somewhat novel solutions to somewhat novel problems (more in the 10 percent category than 10x), are likely to comprise the bulk of your internal innovation projects. Though incremental, these *little i* innovation efforts can be important for cumulative impact.

It is worth noting that you may be accustomed to thinking of innovation *horizons* in terms of how long something takes to develop. The trouble with an overly time-based approach is that something you assume (or hope) is way out there might well become rapidly accessible, with some effort, resourcing, and prioritization. Conversely, it might take considerably longer than you anticipate. Either way, horizons considered on the basis of novelty rather than time frame help you assess the risks involved and understand whether your organization or the innovation ecosystem has the talent, resources, and risk appetite to take on different projects instead of focusing on whether you have the patience to wait until a project is completed.

Managers considering their investments in innovation can plot and visualize their innovation projects across this problem/solution matrix. At the frontier, the matrix has several key zones of novelty (see figure 1.3), each of which includes different types of innovation projects with their own unique characteristics and risks, and each of which will benefit from a range of different, specialized resources, and opportunities for experimentation that might be provided internally or from the innovation ecosystem.

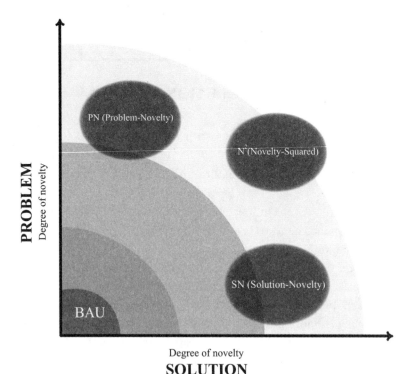

Figure 1.3
Zones out to the innovation frontier's far foundation.

PN Is High Problem-Novelty, SN Is Solution-Novelty, and N^2 is Novelty-Squared

The first zone we refer to as **PN** is at the end of the vertical problem-novelty axis. This is where your organization is working on projects exploring how existing solutions can be applied to the new problems it faces. While you might do this internally, we often find ideas in this zone coming from units assigned to tech scouting, such as those deployed by Belinda into the field to find solutions to some of her organization's newest mission challenges, with her teams looking for existing technologies outside the organization that might be repurposed internally. The innovation approach pioneered by our MIT colleague Eric von Hippel—referred to as *open innovation*—often involved end users proposing existing solutions (or small adaptations) to their own novel problems (rather than waiting for large organizations to guess what they might want solved).[15] While the solutions might not be new, the users might apply them to problems that the producers did not anticipate.

The second zone—**SN**—sits at the bottom right corner, at the end of the horizontal solution-novelty axis. Here, projects explore ideas with emerging or frontier solutions applied to existing problems. In this zone, your organization focuses on solutions that may be distant from its existing skill set and resources or that take a different approach than the company has explored previously. That said, corporate R&D departments or governmental *S&T* teams may have high-novelty solutions to their organization's existing problems on the agenda.

The third and final zone in our diagram is where high SN meets high PN (i.e., N^2, novelty-squared). It is often characterized by areas of emerging technology, also known as *deep tech*. This includes breakthroughs such as *quantum computing* that has held promise for decades but is increasingly considered to be essential to the future of computing, albeit with significant risks to resolve before it will likely reach widespread commercial relevance, as they can use quantum mechanics to solve incredibly complex calculations. While the details are beyond the scope of this book (or indeed its authors!), what is important is that if and when a reliable, so-called fault-tolerant quantum computer is constructed at an adequate scale to do meaningful calculations, it will be able to solve a wide range of problems that had hitherto been ignored as being too hard and intractable. The development of quantum computing is an N^2 zone project as it will enable new problems and thus new business opportunities, as well as challenges in national security (given that a quantum computer is likely to be able to decrypt most of the information that is encrypted with current cryptographic methods) as much as new solutions.

Projects across the innovation horizon can involve PN projects, SN projects, or N^2 projects. In all three instances, innovation ecosystem engagement is likely to be a valuable source of projects, ones that often provide alternatives (or complements) to internal project activities.

For PN projects, start-ups and other small businesses in the ecosystem that might never have been confronted with your unique problem may be uniquely placed to solve it. Remember the Egyptian start-up Veezeta, founded by Amir Basoum in Cairo (and then expanding to Dubai) to serve the rapidly expanding need for digital health services across the Middle East and North Africa (MENA) region. While the problem Amir was solving was new to the MENA region—that is, online medicine—the solutions he drew upon were reasonably well understood, and he was able to customize them in ways that uniquely served the market. For corporations seeking to find new customer market segments, especially in regions with distinctive opportunities and changing needs, it is important to engage with emerging ecosystems just as Google has through its work across Africa from Nairobi (Kenya) to Accra (Ghana) to Johannesburg (South Africa).

In contrast, for SN projects, there might be a different group of stakeholders in the ecosystem with potentially novel solutions. For example, universities might focus on cutting-edge research that may form the foundation of powerful new solutions that could be relevant to your well-understood problems. University faculty are focused on novelty, rewarded for it through the publication or (increasingly) the patent process, and they have a continuous stream of motivated PhD students to support them. The latter may even *spin out* such ideas from the research labs into start-up ventures.

As an illustration, let's visit the innovation ecosystem in Halifax, Nova Scotia, perched on the Atlantic coast of Canada. There, a team led by Rick MacDonald, a self-professed maker and tinkerer, with degrees in physics and decades of ocean experience, founded a venture called CarteNav in 2002. After twenty years of activity integrating novel ideas into *intelligence, surveillance, and reconnaissance* (ISR) software, from the seabed to the land and air, the team was asked by the new Centre for Ocean Ventures and Entrepreneurship (COVE) to partner on its Digital Harbor initiative. This project aimed to map Halifax Harbor, one of the deepest and largest natural harbors in the world.

Given the local expertise of CarteNav, COVE didn't have to look far to find novel solutions to a known problem. Indeed, the capability the

partners developed was considered sufficiently exciting to marine naviga-
tion that, when NATO was looking for a North American location for its
new Defense Innovation Accelerator for the North Atlantic (DIANA) network, it selected Halifax as a place that might attract the next generation of
innovators solving traditional problems of marine and maritime security.

Last, for N^2 projects like those in quantum computing, companies like
IBM and Microsoft recognize them as essential to their future growth. While
quantum research can be identified in innovation ecosystems around the
world (wherever there are leading universities with strong research traditions in atomic physics), it is only in a few that we also find quantum
engineers, the semiconductor expertise and infrastructure that is needed
to build new quantum chips, and the investors who are willing to explore
investments at this distant frontier of knowledge that is hard to understand
and even harder to assess.

Surprising to some, Copenhagen—the beautiful city in northern Europe
—has emerged as a key ecosystem in quantum computing. It has a storied
history of physics, including the important contributions of Professor Niels
Bohr, who founded the Institute for Theoretical Physics in 1921 (which is
now named after him) at the University of Copenhagen, and who won
the Nobel Prize in Physics a year later. This has led to deep expertise in
quantum physics that has been boosted by attracting leading US physi-
cists as well as engineering talent. But the real boost has recently come
from a dedicated commitment by the government and the well-funded
Novo Nordisk Foundation to support quantum engineering and the creation of a quantum foundry. This foundry brings specialized infrastructure to match the specialized talent and offers a place for funding and
experimentation.

Complementing the foundation's resources is a government National
Quantum Strategy laying out the country's focus and prioritization of
quantum computing. In addition, the ecosystem has attracted Microsoft's
industrial sponsorship of research at the University of Copenhagen. These
elements of a small but burgeoning ecosystem in the N^2 zone have started
to see the creation of several quantum-focused start-up ventures, from
Molecular Quantum Solutions to Hafnium Labs. Additionally, this ecosystem is starting to support partnerships and international collaborations
with quantum start-ups from other ecosystems including, for example,
Atlantic Quantum in Boston.

Supporting Access to Specialized Resources

If innovation ecosystems support novelty, they also provide the highly specialized resources needed to initiate the innovation process and to drive it forward along the path from ideation, through prototyping, pilots, and commercialization, to impact. The further the innovation strays away from BAU, the harder it becomes for organizations to obtain these often unusual resources, especially for SN and N^2 projects. Conversely, participants (from any stakeholder group) in ecosystems can exchange resources across many ideas and projects because they specialize in innovation, often in unique fields (such as autonomous vehicles in Singapore, quantum in Copenhagen, the ocean in Halifax, cybersecurity in Tel Aviv, or fintech and *healthtech* in Cairo).

Our work illustrates three key types of specialized resources in innovation ecosystems that are especially useful to large organizations when they are attempting to work on high-novelty innovations: specialized talent, specialized stage-specific risk capital, and specialized infrastructure. These are three sorts of resources that might internally be poorly matched to a particular innovation project and are hard to rapidly bring in-house. Instead, the innovation ecosystem is an alternative resource pool.

Specialized talent. By specialized talent, we mean the people with the right, often rare knowledge and skills needed to develop an idea: people like Rick at CarteNav with over twenty years of experience in the ocean sector. Although expertise in a specific discipline is essential to creating viable solutions to particular problems (such as in medicine for new treatments or computer science for digital technology), so is a deep familiarity with the potential customer or end user. Successful ecosystems often have a density of problem owners, from doctors to special forces teams to civil servants to insurance agents. They are often the innovators and entrepreneurs who lead ideas through the bumpy first stages of the journey toward impact.

Ecosystems often serve as a nexus for service providers, whose insights can make a difference, especially in the messy, uncertain early days of the innovation journey. These include IP and VC lawyers, who can draw up patents and investment *term sheets* with speed and efficiency; clinical trial designers, who can help new teams determine how to design a regulatory pathway; or people who know the ins and outs of local government and can help obtain permits for pilot facilities. Large organizations shifting toward different innovation priorities often do not have these experts in-house, as their own internal teams focus on supporting BAU or 10 percent innovation projects.

Specialized finance. Specialized *risk capital* includes investors who focus on very novel, risky ideas and provide financing in a staged manner that matches the level of risk and experimentation entrepreneurial teams will need to undertake. These sorts of funding structures and the investors who make those decisions are not easily replicated inside large organizations. The innovators and entrepreneurs also need more than just adequate access to capital. Investment in early-stage ideas and teams especially requires understanding the risks associated with novel markets and novel S&T insights, and a willingness to make decisions about ideas and people with very limited data.

As a result, early-stage investors in innovation ecosystems are often highly specialized by type, by stage of innovation, and by industry sector. Greater Boston, for example, has one of the highest concentrations of VC firms with expertise supporting teams that are developing biomedical technology. These include Flagship Pioneering, Third Rock, Engine Ventures, and Atlas Ventures. Similarly in climate change, investors have emerged with specialized skills in selecting and supporting novel ideas in carbon capture, battery storage technology, and even fusion. Even though this is a novel problem area with novel solutions, investors have already become colocated in ecosystems from Greater Boston and Silicon Valley to London and Berlin. These skills and the associated investment approaches are often hard to replicate within large organizations, except sometimes within *corporate venture capital* (CVC) units (which we explore in chapter 4).

Specialized infrastructure. Last, by infrastructure, we are not referring to roads, railways, airports, and internet networks (important as they are) but rather specialized offerings, such as development or test facilities that allow for testing and piloting novel ideas. These include cleanrooms and atomic scale microscopes for quantum computer chips, clinical trial sites for pharmaceuticals, open fields for drones, and *fabs* for prototyping semiconductor materials.

Having the ability to rapidly demonstrate ideas in the lab and then at the scale of a prototype or pilot is essential to any innovation team.

However, building such equipment from scratch is time-consuming, costly (an Atomic Force Microscope can cost over a million dollars to buy, install, and staff), and complicated to run.

When our MIT School of Engineering colleague Professor Vladmir Bulovic (Vlad to most of his colleagues) visits our classes, he describes his entrepreneurial journey as taking ideas—that range from quantum dot displays to solar cells made from transparent nanomaterials—from his research lab to scale in the economy. He reminds our students that it can often take almost $2 million and two years simply to replicate the results he has generated in the lab—due to the complexity of building the experimental infrastructure to produce and analyze nanostructured materials from scratch—before beginning to scale up production for industrial purposes.

Innovation ecosystems like Paris (France), Heidelberg (Germany), and Lausanne (Switzerland) have gone some way to solving this problem through organizations like LabCentral, BioLabs, and SuperLab Suisse. These provide easy and cost-effective access to *wet lab* infrastructure—the costly and complex spaces where scientists in white lab coats conduct experiments. These new service providers have pioneered a coworking approach, making lab benches available on a monthly basis, akin to a gym membership, in spaces that range from the gritty, industrial former Polaroid Lab in Greater Boston's Kendall Square to the historic, elegantly columned Hotel-Dieu space in the heart of Paris nestled up against the fabled Notre-Dame Cathedral.

Other ecosystems like Copenhagen and Taiwan are now leading in providing infrastructure in quantum and semiconductors, respectively. The prices of these facilities have traditionally been prohibitive for start-up ventures that would have to commit to renting large spaces on a multiyear lease, and even for large corporations, getting access to facilities for novel innovation projects can be difficult in-house. Back on our own campus, Vlad has done likewise by creating the magnificent MIT.nano space. Tucked away behind the iconic MIT dome, this shared facility provides nanoscale fabrication cleanrooms, as well as characterization facilities such as electron microscopes and atomic force microscopes. It is also open to start-ups and large corporations for reasonable fees and with simple contracts, not just university researchers.

Large pharmaceutical companies like Roche, J&J, and Takeda find participating in spaces like LabCentral to be valuable as a way to tap into the infrastructure and, importantly, the life science entrepreneurs who work there. Similarly, for large corporations like Analog Devices, Dow Chemical Company, DSM, and IBM Research, working alongside MIT.nano offers the chance to meet the next generation of experts, test their own equipment, and run their own projects with cutting-edge technicians, while also being embedded with students who represent the next generation of talent.[16]

In Halifax, similarly specialized resources are developing around the ocean economy.[17] Testbeds like Stella Maris—a subsea platform, dockside testing area, and twenty-four-hour data portal—provide a place and tools to rapidly test, develop, and verify ideas in harsh marine environments. It's funded by the Canadian government and the province of Nova Scotia to support advanced ocean technology development. Additionally, the Digital Harbor project we previously described provides a digital sea vessel-testing environment. These unique resources, all gathered in one place, have attracted large organizations like IBM and Thales—a defense, aerospace, and security-focused global corporation that supports, among others, the Royal Canadian Navy—to the Halifax ecosystem.

Enabling Experimentation and Reducing Risk

Experimentation is also a "superpower" of the innovation ecosystem—supporting entrepreneurs and mature organizations in propelling their novel projects forward through efficient learning cycles of experimentation and evaluation in ways that are hard to accomplish in larger, more mature organizations.

Stepping back, we have already described how the innovation journey is fraught with risk. Whether the idea is a bold over-the-horizon effort that pushes the boundary and generates new solutions—like Climeworks in Zurich, which scales direct air capture of carbon dioxide—or endeavors like Vezeeta in Cairo that solve new problems and thus change consumers' medical experience, or teams like CarteNav in Halifax that transform ocean surveillance, the early stages of innovation are risky because they have never been done quite this way before. For teams working on projects like this, the risks of PN and SN projects mean that they must wrestle with at least four types of risk:

- Technical risks: Whether the technology will work in the real world
- Production risks: Whether the solution can be produced at scale reliably, consistently, and for reasonable cost

- Regulatory risks: Whether the solution can comply with legal frame-works and the team can navigate the approval process
- Market risks: Whether customers adopt the product and on what time scale (the usual sense of *product/market fit*)

We have observed and analyzed the experimental journeys of hundreds of innovators like these, especially in start-up ventures, comparing those happening in innovation ecosystems and those in more spartan settings with fewer stakeholders and less substantial shared resources. Such ventures reveal how ecosystems help innovators to manage risk and to examine the ways in which large organizations might use ecosystems to support internal and external experimentation activities across their innovation portfolio.

We have found that innovation ecosystems are places where innova-tion teams get the strongest support for experimenting: teams that can break risks into manageable pieces and run experiments find a range of specialized resources in the ecosystem—outlined above—to support them. By breaking the innovation process down into a series of *innovation cycles* and efficiently gathering resources to test their ideas, innovators and their partners can save money, time, and disappointment. In an ecosystem set-ting, entrepreneurs can more rapidly do tests, gather information, learn, and evaluate compared to those elsewhere who operate without ecosystem support. The reason for this is that experiments, especially those at the early stages of innovation when uncertainty is at its highest, require rapid and low friction access to specialized resources. Because innovation ecosystems support strong personal relationships and even interdependency, both peo-ple and resources can be rapidly shared, information can be exchanged, and, in the event of failure, resources can be redeployed, and people can find other innovation projects to join.

A case in point is Formula 1 (F1) racing and its innovation ecosystem in and around the UK's Silverstone track. The expertise in precision engineer-ing, aerodynamic modeling, and rapid production of unique aircraft that built up during World War II, along with the disused airfields that were repurposed as racetracks, has drawn seven of F1's development teams to be closely colocated in this small, leafy part of Britain (alongside Formula E teams working on electric racing cars!). These teams have highly sophis-ticated personnel, specialized sources of finance, and most importantly, they have built up critical experimental infrastructure and associated supply chains that can be used and reused in a combination of competitive and cooperative exchange. After experimentation in the innovation ecosystem, the products—those fast F1 cars and the experience of the races—can be delivered globally, at tracks in countries and markets around the world.[18]

The innovation community in effective ecosystems supports not only experimentation for projects but also risk-taking and risk reduction for individuals. As an illustration, imagine founding a quantum computing venture in sunny Florida, where the technology industry is more focused on digital advertising and fintech than far-horizon moonshots. You tell the young PhDs in quantum physics who you are trying to lure to Florida that their chances of success at this boundary-pushing start-up are low. They are taking a risk in joining, but you propose that, with your novel approach to *qubit* design, you have a good chance of success. The PhDs might be forgiven for skepticism: if the project fails, they will either have to relocate or change careers.

Now imagine the conversation if you are based in Vancouver, Canada, a city with a vibrant innovation ecosystem with expertise in quantum computing that has been built up around D-Wave—one of the first quantum computing companies in the world, founded in 1999. Making the case to the new hires is much easier. If they join you and the project fails, they will quickly find other opportunities at companies like 1QBit and Abaqus as well as in university centers such as the Quantum Algorithms Institute. The risk to these people is dramatically reduced.

The clear focus on assessing risk and designing exactly the right experiment to evaluate and reduce it is difficult to do inside a large organization, whose procedures often constrain the types of experiments that innovators can run (and the resources available). Furthermore, the discipline of focused experimentation and evaluation is hard to maintain in the face of internal organizational pressures and distractions. If an experiment is a one-off and fails, there may be no benefits to learning, whereas in an ecosystem, lessons from many different experiments accrue across the community, making each subsequent cycle more effective. As a result, large organizations—public and private—can benefit tremendously from engaging ecosystems to run some of their earliest and most ambitious innovation cycles and as a source of experimentation and learning.

Innovation Ecosystems Everywhere

Innovation ecosystems today support almost every industry. Start-up ventures, risk capital, and universities are developing important and novel ideas in sectors well beyond the digital software start-ups that first breathed life and excitement into Silicon Valley in the last century. Ecosystems around the world now support *deep tech*, including solutions that are based on materials science, hardware engineering, and sophisticated software in AI, encryption as well as *digital tech*. They increasingly specialize in key problem areas that are linked to the unique history and circumstances of the place: from water and food security to healthcare and aging, to defense and security of the oceans, to our infrastructure and our land, and especially our climate. They then support ideation, provide resources, and enable experimentation in a wide range of potential solution domains—from digital to deep tech.

And innovation ecosystems have become essential for large organizations. A sophisticated corporate or government innovation strategy demands engagement with entrepreneurs, universities, and risk capital providers in vibrant ecosystems. Sophisticated leaders in global corporations in a range of sectors, as well as some visionary government leaders, have led the way.

Some organizations have been able to design a strategy that explores a wide range of locations across the world. Others may have reasons to focus more locally, including corporations that are "national" or "regional" champions committed to ecosystems in their particular home location, such as Morocco's OCP, Brazil's Vale mining company, or Britain's BT (formerly British Telecom). All of them have crafted partnerships with ecosystem stakeholders in their home regions or in a set of more distant places to solve their most pressing problems and to ensure that they leverage the wealth of new S&T at the innovation horizon.

Ecosystems offer a wealth of novel ideas that support the goals and priorities of even the largest and most complex organizations. They provide specialized resources for idea generation, prototyping, and commercialization that a single organization, no matter how large it is, will be unlikely to have internally or find too costly to maintain. In innovation ecosystems, you will find people, capital, and infrastructure that are optimized for the early stages in the idea to impact journey, when risks are high, time is short, funds are limited, and speed is essential. Last, ecosystems facilitate the experimental cycles that effectively reduce risk and speed up learning

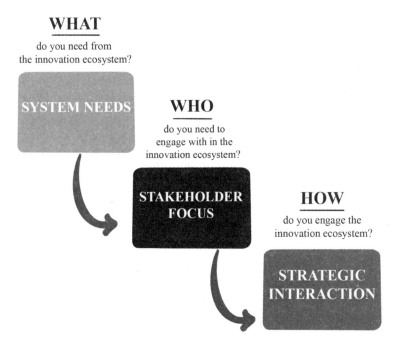

Figure 1.4
The "three questions" (3xQs) of ecosystem engagement—What? Who? How?

and ensure that specialized resources are allocated to the early-stage innovation projects that are so essential to the innovation economy.

Tapping into ecosystems can help you find the ideas, resources, and experiments that are essential for delivering on your top priorities. However, to do this effectively you must answer three questions (see figure 1.4). First, you must know **what** you want from them, second, **who** you want to meet, and third **how** to spend your time and energy wisely. The next three chapters show you how to figure this out, first by understanding the what.

Key Points from Chapter 1: Innovation, Ecosystems, and Their Stakeholders

- *Innovation ecosystems* are place-specific locations (in contrast to dispersed *corporate ecosystems*) that comprise five key stakeholders, that is, entrepreneurs, universities, risk capital providers, corporations, and the government.

- *Innovation ecosystems* are especially rich with the resources that support such innovation activities and are therefore of interest to large organizations.

- *Innovation* is defined as the "process of taking ideas from inception to impact."

- The "process" definition means innovation is a shared journey, not just a single moment of invention by a lone individual.

- The "idea" at "inception" is a proposed match between a problem and a solution: the better this problem/solution match, the better the idea.

- Focused on "impact," the process should result in an outcome that is meaningful to those pursuing such innovation.

- Mapping the problem/solution match to a matrix reveals the novelty (and therefore risk) involved with particular zones in the matrix.

- Large organizations can benefit from engaging these innovation ecosystems by seeking novel ideas, access to specialized resources, and ways of experimenting that reduce risk.

Turning to chapter 2, we will start with the key question of "what" you need from an innovation ecosystem.

2   What You Need from an Innovation Ecosystem

John is an experienced senior executive with a global insurance company. A few years ago, he embarked on an ecosystem fact-finding tour that took him to London, New York, Vancouver, Tokyo, and Singapore, visiting a wide range of start-ups looking for solutions to his most pressing problems.

John checked out companies in London and Vancouver that were developing quantum computing hardware and software. He surmised that faster computers enabled by quantum physics could make the business more efficient at some point in the future, but they were not relevant for his current operations, as even the software solutions were fraught with risk and unlikely to yield benefits for years to come. In New York, Tokyo, and London, he dropped by a few start-ups that piqued his interest: he was most intrigued by those *fintech* ones making payments more customer-friendly or those in the insurance subset (i.e., *insurtech*) reducing premiums for new drivers. The range of ventures and solutions they offered was almost overwhelming. There were so many different alternatives that his head was spinning, and after each meeting, it was hard to clarify the particular follow-up actions he wanted to take with his hosts.

At the end of his travels, John understood why. He was like a tourist on a random walk, taking in the sights, rather than a potential future resident scouting for a comfortable home base. As he reflected on his whirlwind tour, he realized that he needed to return to his team and define the problems that required innovation to solve and the solutions that were missing from his current portfolio of activities. Was still-experimental quantum computing something the firm needed to worry about in the early 2020s to remain competitive? Did it need to move rapidly into new areas of fintech and the emerging field of *insurtech*?

Many leaders, like John, confront the embarrassment of tech riches offered by innovation ecosystems and do not know where to start. And yet they race off anyway, tasked by a superior to "reach out," to "build an innovation lab to engage the ecosystem," to "spearhead an innovation initiative," or literally to "be at the heart of the ecosystem." These senior leaders have rarely defined what success looks like or how it fits into their business strategy. They set their teams up for frustration and failure, and their organizations for reputational harm.

This is not to say innovation tourism has no value. But getting results from any engagement with an ecosystem depends on the answer to this question: *what* is your team, your company, or your organization trying to accomplish from engagement?

To answer this question, you need a clear and complete map of your organization's innovation portfolio—detailing both internal and external projects—and how these align with your innovation strategy. Through our work with various organizations, we have developed a four-step process for creating this map. The map will help you look past the shiny surface of new technologies to see how they might help you achieve your business goals, and in what time period, or to learn how the same technologies may threaten your current operations or open up new opportunities to solve important novel problems. You will have a tool to understand the gaps in your portfolio and develop a grounded perspective for making decisions about where to engage, with whom, and how. With this map in hand, you will be able to identify the priorities you are most likely to address effectively within an innovation ecosystem.

Step 1: Create an Inventory of Your Current Innovation Projects

Determining what you might want from an innovation ecosystem starts with a complete-as-possible accounting of your current innovation projects, all those your company is pursuing, both internally and externally. By corralling information about these disparate activities in one place, you will create a single, shared understanding of your innovation efforts, much as an investor maps out their financial portfolio.

A senior leader—such as a chief technology officer, chief science adviser, head of R&D, or innovation champion—may commission this work and control the resources. However, many people in the organization need to contribute and recognize that such sharing does not necessarily imply a desire to control each and every project. They can report on all their projects, where the work is happening (internally or externally), and the budgets that support them.

In the private sector, this information tends to come from a few key areas:

- *R&D*, which may be running projects internally or externally (e.g., under the auspices of a university relationship manager or a partnership lead working with partners large and small on a range of R&D projects)
- business units, which may be engaged in "little i" projects close to BAU
- marketing, which might be exploring innovation with the next generation of customers
- *CVC* or similar units that might be exploring external equity investments in potential "Big I" projects
- innovation teams, *intrapreneurship*, or corporate entrepreneurship units that are developing new ideas internally

A large mining company we worked with (let's call it MiningCorp) assembled its portfolio by working closely with the R&D group focused on exploration, and with the teams developing "mine of the future" projects involving things like digital twin technology. Information also came from the company's CVC unit and the teams that worked with university researchers and key suppliers.

In the public sector, it can be harder to find out what is taking place under the broad banner of innovation. Chances are that the department or agency has never tracked all its disparate projects as a portfolio, partly because the structure of their budgets makes this difficult. Meanwhile, funds may be earmarked for specific activities or shared projects with another agency, without specifying they are for innovation, potentially making these funds harder to track.

Navigating this labyrinth may require a more hands-on approach. A senior leader like Belinda, our European government executive, convened a small team to scour the agency's finances and work assignments to find out who was working on projects that could be broadly classified as innovation, even if they weren't labeled as such.

While this seems like mundane work, it is important. The information you need may be fragmented, and project owners might resist sharing it, viewing the inventory as an attempt to control their activities or those of their colleagues. You will need to navigate these challenges (we'll tell you how later in the book), and it may take considerable time and energy. For example, it took Belinda's colleagues in a neighboring department almost a year to collect data that was good enough to move to Step 2.

Step 2: Map Out Your Existing Innovation Projects

Armed with the information you have gathered in Step 1, you can map your current innovation activities across the "problem/solution" matrix that we presented in chapter 1. One of the benefits of our matrix is that has a place for all forms of innovation. The goal here is to visualize the degree of novelty, along with the problem/solution risk and reward, for each project.

This is a team activity, and some leaders get stuck at this point: one person's high solution-risk innovation can be another's BAU. In fact, the MiningCorp team spent a lot of time arguing about where to place different projects. However, they concluded that they didn't have to be precise, and they were able to reach a consensus about where each project roughly belonged, after sitting in a windowless room together for a day, with a lot of sticky notes and a robust willingness to debate!

Start by determining roughly where each project sits across the three innovation horizons in the matrix, from 10 percent close to BAU, through 2x innovation—representing a significant but more attainable level of impact—out to 10x impact. (Whiteboards or whitewalls with sticky notes are certainly helpful here.) Remember that you are estimating the rewards that you hope to achieve and the risks you are managing.

For projects toward the 10x areas of the innovation matrix, you can also map them to one of the three zones that we set out above—namely the PN zone (existing solutions to novel problems), the SN zone (novel solutions to existing problems), or the N^2 zone (novel solutions to novel problems). You can also cluster them according to the types of problems or solutions they are exploring. This will give you a rough-and-ready map of how your portfolio is allocated and how much of it focuses on the nearer or further horizons. However, for some organizations, especially those with larger innovation portfolios, it is useful to assess the novelty of the solutions and the problems they are exploring in a more granular scale.

For novel solutions, we recommend using the Technology Readiness Level (TRL) schema developed by NASA. The TRL approach identifies nine stages of R&D, beginning with scientific discovery (Level 1) to technology deployment (Level 9).[1] The lower the number, the more novel the current stage of the solution. Your R&D staff may already use this approach to describe the state of their projects.

In terms of our problem/solution matrix, the TRLs map the horizontal solution axis. The earliest TRL (i.e., starting with TRL 1, scientific discovery) would be out at the far end, at the furthest horizon on the right, with the greatest SN. By TRL 3, a solution has an experimental *proof of concept* in the lab. At TRL 5, there is a large-scale *prototype* in the real-world environment (i.e., out of the lab and into the field). The highest TRLs (i.e., culminating with TRL 8 with a system completed and manufacturing developed, and, finally TRL 9, deployment of technology proven in the field) would be closer to BAU on the horizontal axis, with the lowest SN.

For the team at MiningCorp, a TRL 1 project includes scientific research on the geology of new rock formations (i.e., highly novel because it hasn't been done before). In contrast, a TRL 7 project might be demonstrating the application of robots for extracting ore in an operational environment (i.e., a solution new to them but not cutting edge or "new to the world"). In between, projects included an entirely new digital twin of an existing mine that was being developed (and had reached TRL 5 and was being validated in an operationally relevant environment) to allow the company to develop simulations of new extraction approaches and to determine how other, much more incremental, innovations might impact overall productivity. Another project focused on new water treatment methods was still at TRL 4, being validated with a small-scale lab prototype.

The problem/solution matrix also adds an important dimension to the linear, solution-focused TRLs, in that some of the projects moving from scientific discovery to tech deployment will be at different levels of PN. For example, some will be addressing existing problems, while others will focus on problems that are otherwise unknown (or novel) to you and your organization.

To approximate PN, you can distinguish between problems that are new to the users within your organization or to your existing customers (low novelty), and problems that are truly new to the world (high novelty). Also, think about how well your organization understands the problem, the people who will benefit from the solution, and their preferences when it comes to selecting among different possible solutions (including the price and a set of solution characteristics). The less you know about the users, the more novel the problem is, at least for your organization. Such assessments may be less fine-grained than the TRL schema for solutions, but the problem axis is sometimes helpfully referred to as market readiness with projects from low levels of market (or problem) readiness to higher levels when the market, the context, and its customers are very well understood.

Applying this to MiningCorp, a novel problem where it might apply its existing solutions could be leveraging its extraction expertise to other ores, such as minerals that have recently become "critical" due to national security or the energy transition. Lithium is a good example of such critical minerals where incumbent iron-ore mining firms have much to offer, but where firms must appreciate the needs of a new group of customers and different market conditions (a problem of medium novelty).

Some novel problems may be truly new to the world and have high PN, such as the desire to operate on Mars. Here, a problem owner like NASA may turn to incumbent miners—such as those in Perth, Western Australia—who are used to operating in remote, red-soiled terrain with harsh climates to develop an innovation project in the N^2 zone—with high novelty on both the problem and solution axes.[2] We have also found MiningCorp working on novel problems related to the environmental footprint of their mining operations—working to meet new regulatory and shareholder requirements, thus seeking solutions (new and existing) to this new problem.

Two last refinements of your map are to note the scale and scope of your projects.

On scale, we suggest visualizing each project's scale with a circle so that its relative size represents the relative resources—such as budgets or headcount—of each project. Whatever the formal strategy, the distribution and scale of the projects in different parts of the matrix represent what your large organization is doing on innovation.

On scope, separate out (visually) which projects are being undertaken in-house and which involve partnerships or contracts with external parties. This additional layer of analysis opens a window into the balance of internal versus external innovation efforts and where in the world your innovative efforts are happening.

MiningCorp was able to see which of its high-novelty solutions were being generated by its R&D group internally, versus those further along the solution axis, in partnership with universities. Leaders also identified the

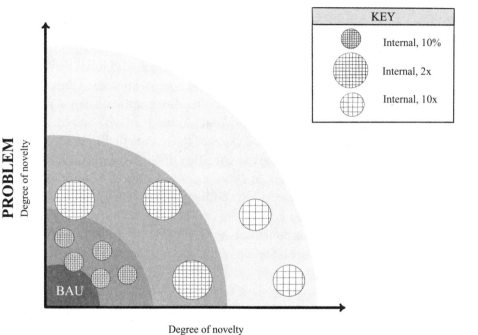

Figure 2.1
Map your innovation portfolio on the problem/solution matrix.

novel problems being tackled by existing business units compared to innovations for new problems being generated by the team responsible for new
business, or through relationships with external start-ups. By including the
efforts of the tech-scouting team (high on the vertical problem axis, in the
PN zone) alongside those of the R&D unit (in the SN zone on the horizontal
axis) in the portfolio, the organization could see different avenues of innovation (figure 2.1).

By mapping out its innovation efforts, MiningCorp also noticed that
its CVC efforts were missing in their more traditional portfolio mapping
exercises. Each external venture investment should appear on the prob-
lem/solution matrix, out on the horizon at various points (e.g., PN, SN,
or N^2) alongside the other innovation projects by the R&D and tech-
scouting teams. With that, the MiningCorp team could see how much was
being committed to external start-up activities, how this complemented

its internal efforts, and, importantly, where in the world these ventures seemed to be concentrated.

The extra level of detail provided by mapping external, as well as internal projects (noting their geographic locations), helps to connect external ecosystem innovation activities with the core internal innovation portfolio of your organization. Unless leaders know the scope of these external projects and the potential diversity they bring to the portfolio—and include them in planning conversations—external efforts (whether from CVC or university relationships) are easy to cut when times are tough. Such projects may be seen as a fashion or fad of a particular leader or team, or as disconnected from the organization's business strategy. On the other hand, when carefully integrated into a complete innovation portfolio, external ecosystem engagement is more likely to be viewed as essential to business and mission priorities, with the relevant teams held accountable for their contributions.

Step 3: Reconfigure the Portfolio to Match Your Innovation Strategy

Your portfolio map is a shared reference point for innovation across your organization. And it is a starting point for shaping and prioritizing the organization's projects, based on what it wants to accomplish with its innovation strategy overall.

A full discussion of this essential work is not possible in this book for every zone of the portfolio, from BAU out to the innovation horizon. Because we are concerned with helping you identify what you want from the external ecosystem, we focus here on the rationalization and reconfiguration of your innovation portfolio at the further horizons—from 2x to 10x impact—where ambitious novel ideas anticipated and where you are most likely to need external resources from an ecosystem. However, we recommend you evaluate your entire portfolio to answer the "what" question most clearly.

When MiningCorp went through this process, it paid particular attention to projects beyond the 10 percent near horizon and instead looked out at farther horizons, where their portfolio had a large number of disparate projects and where the leadership team felt the strategy was unclear but the importance was high. Without a focused approach to the future—both novel problems and novel solutions—the leadership team felt they might fall behind competitors and miss out on significant opportunities. They were also convinced that there was an opportunity for effective ecosystem engagement to support their far-horizon activities because their existing, albeit fragmented, external efforts had potential (especially some of the ventures that they had seen through their investment activities). That said, the MiningCorp team knew there was work ahead to build a really effective strategy for their horizon activities and a chance to optimize their use of ecosystems.

In the furthest horizon part of the portfolio, we find that organizations must often cut, expand, or adapt projects for three reasons:

- First, they find *gaps* they need to explore but have no or too few projects: they need to broaden their exploration of the problem or solution space.

- Second, they find that they need more resources, and more specialized ones that are not available in-house, to deliver on their project goals.

- Third, they find that they have not created opportunities to explore the whitespace beyond their existing imaginations and beyond their current portfolio.

Let's first consider the gaps. When you look at your portfolio, you see your organization's commitment to innovation. It illustrates what you are really trying to achieve or at least what your organization is committing its time, people, and money to undertaking. However, you may find that these commitments don't match the formal strategy.

If the strategy calls for a strong commitment to solving new customer challenges by adapting existing technologies, and yet the portfolio has little or no activity in the PN zone (existing solutions to novel problems), your efforts are misaligned. Similarly, you have a mismatch if you want to deploy new technologies in your well-understood markets but have not invested many resources in SN zone (novel solutions to existing problems) internally or externally. Last, you are misaligned if your organization has noted and committed to the strategic role of *deep tech* to address new business opportunities and challenges but you have few or no projects in the N^2 zone (novel solutions to novel problems).

Every organization is different, with different needs for novelty and innovation. While there is no such thing as an optimal or "balanced portfolio" for innovation, many organizations we meet feel a strong imperative to allocate time and energy to the long-term, imagined futures of important

2x and 10x innovation, and yet they are pulled back into the urgent 10 percent horizon that addresses known business needs. We have found that organizations typically underinvest in innovation at these further-out horizons. Their desired portfolio—one that can achieve their strategic innovation goals—is not exactly what they have mapped in Steps 1 and 2 above. It needs to be rebalanced, with more investment in higher-novelty problem or solution spaces. As previously noted, these are where we see the opportunities for external ecosystem engagement due to the greater novelty of solutions and problems available there.

Working with your team, and based on your shared strategic views of the future opportunities and challenges your organization will be facing, you will likely have a sense of the portfolio you need and where the gaps are. You will see how your resources should be allocated across different parts of the innovation matrix, especially how much more to allocate at the 2x to 10x horizons, and across the frontier zones PN, SN, and N^2.

Take Kristo (let's call him), a senior leader in a defense department of a small NATO member country, with responsibilities for defense investments to build the sorts of capabilities that his country's forces might need. He now has oversight of the activities of the core defense forces, a task he came to after longtime experience in a range of defense R&D and innovation programs. For decades, the role of defense—especially in western Europe and North America—was relatively stable. As a result, Kristo and the defense department more broadly were committed to a low-novelty portfolio, with only limited allocations to riskier, novel horizons. Such novel investments were often confined to R&D labs and were distant from the end users.

But as competition and conflict have increased in the world, Kristo and his team see a greater need for capabilities in, and control over, emerging technologies (such as quantum computing, which affects cybersecurity) even though their country could not possibly develop all of its own technologies alone. Interestingly, at the same time as Kristo's team is worrying about quantum computing, so are the leaders in multinational pharmaceutical companies. The attention to medicinal chemistry and protein folding by new companies—from Google's DeepMind to Vancouver-based Good Chemistry, Swiss-based Terra Quantum, and Qubit Pharma in Paris—suggests that big pharma needs to shift its portfolio. Kristo's portfolio needs to shift to higher-novelty horizons, not only for new projects that apply novel technologies (like quantum sensing) to traditional problems, but also to solve entirely new military challenges by taking advantage of existing commercial products. Similarly, in the pharmaceutical industry, we are seeing a redistribution of longer-term R&D on the high-novelty horizon to new types of modeling approaches and a wealth of novel tools.

For our colleagues at MiningCorp, global trends have also forced a shift in resources toward the higher-novelty horizon. The company is looking for ways to mitigate its effect on the climate while navigating complex geopolitics and rapid adoption in its industry of digital technologies and robotics. It is shifting its portfolio to solving more of these novel problems.

Additionally, large organizations in the private sector, and especially the public sector, now want to give their horizon efforts realistic budgets, rather than making aspirational promises that funding will be provided sometime in the future, which likely will never materialize. This approach is especially common in the public sector, where political leaders balance rhetoric about the future with the reality of limited budgets. MiningCorp leaders have made difficult decisions to reduce investment elsewhere (typically by reallocating from the 10 percent projects) to make space, time, and resources available. And Kristo and his colleagues in the defense department have been trying to identify cuts to the urgent operational needs of frontline forces to allocate funds for investments in innovation. These investments will be essential for supporting national defense and security goals in the future. This is not an easy task, but it is nearly impossible without some form of portfolio planning, like the approach we advocate.

Even when organizations have some projects out toward the 10x horizon, they need to see whether their efforts are configured broadly enough to account for the novelty that is a key characteristic of the further horizon, and to account for the higher rates of failure that come with riskier projects. MiningCorp found that by working with a very narrow set of approaches to autonomous robotics, it was missing opportunities to explore new ones that were becoming available in start-ups and university labs. And it had not fully committed to a program of new, more environmentally friendly extraction technologies that might allow them to move mining rare earths and critical minerals to more local regions, instead of keeping operations in China, for example.

Kristo had a similar observation: his team recognized that new digital tech—ranging from scheduling algorithms and image analysis to applying new *AI large language models* (LLMs) to satellite data—could be profoundly important to the goals of his large but budget-constrained department. And yet the emphasis in the innovation activities to date had largely been on building up some limited internal software capabilities, and on moving the more traditional support functions (e.g., human resources) to the cloud. He had a clear gap in the sorts of 2x projects that could transform operational activities with the exception of one or two small projects undertaken by entrepreneurial members of his team in a shoestring. And his department was far away from being able to apply LLMs to some of their most important but novel missions (N^2 zone types of projects).

Even the executives in some of the big pharma companies we have worked with—who have long been used to shifting the allocation of their far-horizon resources (e.g., SN projects) from one disease and one type of therapeutic approach to another—were finding it difficult to shift into the entirely new domain of DL, AI-enabled models, and the distant potential of quantum software.

Many organizations are like MiningCorp, and many leaders confront the challenges that Kristo unearthed in his portfolio efforts: they have ventured toward the horizon and picked one or two projects that often lack variety, rather than undertaking a wider exploration. This is understandable, as variety is costly and the horizon is wide. That said, organizations need variety the most when the risks are high, as many ideas and approaches won't pan out.

Ecosystems Offer More Variety Than Companies May Have Access to Internally

Turning to the second reason leaders need to recalibrate and reconfigure their far-horizon portfolio—beyond filling gaps and widening the scope of novel projects—is to ensure they have the necessary resources to be effective. We find that organizations often don't. For projects essential to their strategic goals on the horizon, they may lack the relevant technical skills and the infrastructure for experimentation. Many organizations—public and private—also lack the experimentation culture and commitment to test and learn. As we mentioned earlier, MiningCorp was using new sensor technology to build a digital twin of its mine so that it could experiment with the digital version of its real-world mine. However, the company had fallen behind the best digital practices in other industrial sectors, in part because it had not invested enough in digital expertise (such as the machine learning part of AI). It also lacked a full experimental testbed for such new technologies and was hampered by a lack of experimentation culture that supported learning and rapid cycles of innovation.

These horizon activities might be good areas for ecosystem engagement because, as we've noted, large organizations may not have been able to build up sufficient internal expertise, testing infrastructure, and experimentation capacity in a new technical area. A lack of the right resources in-house is an opportunity for ecosystem engagement, say in the SN zone (novel solutions to existing problems). Or for many organizations, the challenge of horizon projects (especially in the PN zone) may be difficulty in finding and engaging a new group of customers with different profiles than their existing clientele. Moreover, when exploring new customer needs, your organization may want to run experiments that are difficult to do internally because they are off-brand, require permission, or are otherwise sensitive.

If the organization shifts these projects to an external ecosystem, say in the PN zone (existing solutions to novel problems), it can observe experiments without running into reputational risk (of failure) or bureaucratic obstacles. And by keeping the experiments out in the ecosystem, you might also avoid signaling to competitors which areas of novel technology or which novel customers (or which potential enemies) you are most interested in, thus limiting the insights you provide into your strategic plans.

Watch for Blind Spots

The underlying assumption of a portfolio that includes both internal system activities and external ecosystem engagement is that you have a deep and thorough understanding of the trends shaping the novelty of both problems and solutions. But you will need to challenge that assumption because novelty is about the unexpected as much as the expected trends. The third reason to reconsider your portfolio is therefore to ensure that you consider the *unknown unknowns* over the horizon, not simply the known unknowns.[3]

Organizations face a daunting innovation landscape that gets vaguer and more uncertain as you move out from BAU toward the riskiest frontier: evolving customer needs, emerging technologies, geopolitical shifts that render some markets and technologies off-limits, or sudden supply chain shocks. The speed at which everything changes can leave organizations subject to strategic surprise—and blind spots in their portfolios. These blind spots are whitespace that organizations might leave empty for lack of foresight, knowledge, or resources. Strategic surprise can be unsettling. It can harm corporate profits or challenge governments' ability to maintain public health or national security. Ecosystem engagement can come in useful here too.

A traditional solution to anticipating blind spots was to allow individual researchers and scientists their own time to explore the innovation frontier. Organizations such as 3M and later Google would give select individuals one day a week to investigate unknowns in the library, on the laptop or in the lab, to be more creative and explore novel areas of inquiry that maximize long-term impact.[4]

Today, this type of research can also be fruitfully accomplished within an innovation ecosystem. Ecosystems provide a window into the unexpected and the intriguing—less through specific and well-defined projects but more by gaining inspiration through the flow of novel ideas. While this might appear remarkably similar to the innovation tourism we previously cautioned against, well-curated and inspiring visits turn ecosystem touring from mere tourism to tech scouting with a specific purpose. When configured around a big question or talks with experts on the innovation horizon—asking not only what they are doing but also why they are doing it—these visits can help give more shape and color to white space. As such, these activities should be in the portfolio as they takes time, attention, and resources out in one or more of the zones on the matrix but especially the N^2 zone.

Step 4: Get Specific About "What" You Need

As you reshape your innovation portfolio, you will be forced to get specific about what you need the innovation ecosystem to deliver for each project across the horizon(s). Novel solutions? Attention to a novel problem? Specific resources—specialized talent, unique testing infrastructure? Opportunities to experiment? What you decide will be the ultimate answer to the question we asked at the beginning of the chapter: **what** do you need from an innovation ecosystem?

As you work to pull your innovation portfolio together to clarify your strategic approach to the innovation ecosystem, you want to be specific and consider the three zones in the outer edges of the matrix, which, for the reasons mentioned above, may need to be filled. Regardless of where you most need to reshape your portfolio or how far out on the innovation horizon, you will wish to design and develop innovation projects across each of these three zones. It is projects in these zones that are the answer to the "what" that you want the external innovation ecosystem engagement to deliver.

Let's look at two examples, one from the US Air Force (USAF) and another drawn from our work with several financial services companies, to see how to make these decisions. In the case of the USAF, the team was working at a medium horizon (e.g., 2x) to expand their ability to solve problems using novel digital solutions to improve the operational efficiency of their flight missions. Looking to financial services, we explore a composite example of an organization working at the 10x horizon to understand how innovations in quantum computing impact its business. This includes building an engagement approach to define its necessary interactions to ensure to future success.

We first turn to our colleagues at the USAF, with whom we have worked in many MIT executive programs. Their efforts to get beyond BAU and internal innovation had them looking out to what we call an intermediate 2x horizon. They identified a gap in their software expertise to solve a range of existing and novel problems the staff were regularly facing in their flight missions—in combat, training, and logistics and support. They were stuck in a rut working with large *prime* contractors (a corporate in our language) or relying on their internal R&D units, but this traditional approach had narrowed the USAF solution space, causing them to gain limited novelty from their external corporate partner. Additionally, the solutions were coming in slowly with little or no experimentation as the teams traditionally put forward specifications and then waited (years) for a solution to be delivered. There were also limited opportunities for novel talent to be brought in touch with the USAF. The team determined that they needed to add external ecosystem engagement across all three zones.

As an alternative approach to their PN zone challenges—finding existing solutions to their novel problems—the USAF looked to the Boston ecosystem for existing software development and digital skills to address the new challenges it was facing with coordinating in-flight refueling. They developed a new unit named "Kessel Run" (in a nod to the Star Wars galaxy) to work on engaging new talent to bring established software approaches into new problems.[5] (There were other USAF ecosystem engagements that emphasized emerging 10x technologies, like quantum sensing and future communications, but this was not one of them.) By shifting the project from a traditional internal process or a prime corporate contract to engaging with the external ecosystem, the USAF found the resources and opportunities for rapid experimentation.

To overcome an SN zone gap in their missions (see the zone in the bottom right-hand corner of the matrix in figure 1.3), the USAF hoped to use their own internal R&D capabilities to expand the application of novel digital technologies to fuse data from past missions and from onboard sensors to help pilots make real-time decisions. But in today's more resource-constrained era, gaps were widening, and they realized that external engagement was fruitful. USAF expanded its work at MIT with the creation of an AI accelerator research partnership to build new solutions (referred to as the "Guardian Autonomy" project) via faculty and student research partnerships with aircrew who were the frontline problem owners.

The third area for USAF ecosystem engagement was in the N^2 zone—an area so often associated with gaps and, even when filled, a mismatch in resources that we noted above. Overcoming this often takes a more systematically multistakeholder approach to garner the range of resources that are missing, that is, human capital and effective risk capital, as well as the sort of access to customers, data, and testbeds that allow for rapid testing. In one example, they recognized that they were facing an increasing range of more unstable weather conditions—often driven by climate change—and, at the same time, they had to consider how to deal with more civilian issues of massive forest fires, increased flooding, agricultural disasters, and so forth. While not having a clearly developed solution in hand, they knew that more accurate weather information was possible and might improve their combat missions in a range of hard-to-imagine ways.

To deal with this, the USAF turned to start-up ventures like Clima-Cell (now renamed Tomorrow.io)—a Boston-based start-up with air force founders—which has an approach to gathering weather insights that cleverly combines advanced satellite data with insights gleaned from interference between cellphone towers. Working with the Tomorrow.io team, the USAF was able to take advantage of investments the venture had made in developing weather data solutions for various large organizations. These included the military, insurance companies worried about climate at the macro level, and organizers of outdoor events (such as sports) concerned about weather at the micro level.

The second example we want to share focuses on a composite company in finance that we will call "FinCo" based on a range of different experiences we have had with large financial service sector leaders determining whether and how to respond to opportunities and challenges out at the 10x horizon—mainly focused on the role of *quantum computing*.

The question of "how to deal with quantum" is one we often get asked and one that many large organizations struggle with, especially those who have mainly focused on opportunities from digital tech. In the private sector, leaders don't want to miss out and be surprised if their competitors use quantum computing to build new products and services. In the public and private sectors, government leaders worry about how cryptographic systems will be safeguarded when powerful quantum computers become widely available.

For FinCo, like many organizations, understanding and reacting to the rapid advances in quantum computing (much like advances in other areas of emerging technology) is a context where external ecosystem engagement is likely to be an important strand in their innovation portfolio. But before we dive in, it's worth stepping back and describing in brief what this highly technical field of quantum computing really is and why it has garnered so much interest. At the core, a quantum computer is one that harnesses the qualities of quantum physics to solve problems that are too complex for classical computers. Using *quantum bits* (*qubits*), it will ultimately be able to do so in ways that are faster, more accurate, and almost unimaginably more powerful. When that time comes, organizations that deploy quantum computers will be able to make financial models that are ever more complex and yet rapid, will allow more accurate and sophisticated drug discovery, and—for national security agencies—will allow for even more decryption (rendering current encryption quite vulnerable).[6]

Currently there are a handful of large corporations that build quantum computers—Google and IBM, alongside over 350 start-up ventures.[7] In terms of novelty, quantum computing solutions come in different "flavors" (such as superconducting qubits or those caught in ion traps), with significant uncertainty about which will prove most practical or whether some are better suited to specific problems than others. Most quantum computing efforts are, at the time of writing, around TRL 3 to 4.

Last, the *quantum computing* field requires significant technical talent (with long training in quantum physics and engineering) and specialized resources including facilities for experimenting, making quantum chips, and providing cooling to keep the chips at ultralow temperatures. The sort of novelty and specialization that quantum computing requires can only be found in a handful of ecosystems around the world that have emerged in recent years—Vancouver (since the founding of D-Wave), Toronto, Boston, Oxford, Copenhagen, and Stockholm—but there is certainly a shortage of quantum computing talent (in both science and engineering).

So, imagine FinCo wrestling with how to configure its innovation portfolio at the quantum horizon. How does the company respond, especially when experts are unclear on timelines, milestones, and *use cases*? Mapping their existing activities, our FinCo colleagues had made a foray into this arena by hiring several experts from IBM and elsewhere to help build a quantum-ready strategy. They regularly visited academics in the field across the United States (and to a lesser extent in Europe). They had a few internal projects that mainly tried to map the field and hired external consultants to do something similar. Based on their work so far, FinCo is clear that not only does quantum computing provide an opportunity to run company's existing algorithms more effectively, but it may also offer new modeling opportunities that could result in new products and services. Getting this right could be a source of competitive advantage. However, FinCo also started to realize that quantum computing is also likely to have less desirable consequences, like any technology: for example, the power to render current online digital and data security obsolete.

Looking to that not-too-distant future, FinCo knew its strategy had to harness the same properties of quantum computing to safeguard its data and analytics, in so-called postquantum encryption. Getting this right was, the company decided, not likely to be a source of competitive advantage, but it would likely to expose laggards to liability issues and the loss of customers. Thus, it needed to remain aware of what was happening on the frontier and not get blindsided by sudden decryption advances. Beyond understanding the opportunities posed by quantum computing, the company also realized that talent was in short supply, especially in North America, making it hard to mount an internal effort of any magnitude.

FinCo decided to do most of its quantum portfolio in the external innovation ecosystem, aiming for a high degree of novelty and a wide aperture into different quantum solutions—a decision that rested on the lack of talent, difficulty in hiring, and the wide range of novel approaches still in the running. However, the company also needed a significant level of internal expertise so that it could capitalize on the emergence of a commercially reliable and robust quantum computer, as well as explore how quantum computers might shape its most important problems. As a result, FinCo aimed to work closely with some trusted consulting partners and investors and to hire one or two internal experts from the large tech companies.

The bank considered its priorities for engagement across the three zones we have identified. In the PN zone, it already had a project deploying a quantum computing software team to work with partners on some specific problems that have always been impossible for today's digital computers to solve. But the innovation team was worried that this was too narrow an aperture, looking at only one "flavor" of quantum computing. As a result, the team chose to expand their field of view in two ways. First, they solicited new internal problems that the organization might solve using access to some of the newer quantum computing services. Second, they sought to work with another company that had different approaches to quantum computing to try and understand whether these variations mattered.

In the SN zone, FinCo had an internal project that was quite small, in collaboration with a university on building a next-generation quantum computer, which was an exciting, if limited, "pet project" of the R&D unit for several years. The leaders of the innovation portfolio were worried that it was not delivering value given the long timeline to real, commercial results—it was tapping into novelty but with no clear strategic purpose and without the requisite expertise in-house to learn effectively. To address this, the leaders decided to stop this project and refocus its university partnership toward developing more quantum-ready software solutions. This shift would allow them to better understand necessary changes to their software approaches in the future.

Finally, in the N^2 zone, FinCo realized that there might be entirely new start-up businesses that, were they to have quantum computing capabilities, might change how they would serve customers or even who their customers might be. The company realized there might be a blind spot here that was hard to define, but it needed to engage with the ecosystem to at least keep up, in some small way, with rapidly changing developments. As a result, it chose to invest in several start-ups mainly focused on quantum software, based on the expectation that hardware would become more reliably available. The challenge, however, would be to use it well. The company also sought to engage with the wide postquantum encryption community to keep abreast of encryption and decryption challenges. This involved integrating its internal cybersecurity expertise—traditionally quite separate from the company's internal R&D efforts—with the computing and encryption sides of quantum computing.

Last, the bank chose to pursue this strategy across only two innovation ecosystems rather than spreading its effort over the half dozen or so possible locations. This approach allowed it to become more deeply engaged in the community and benefit from its own growing network of relationships and reputation.

Make Strategic Choices

Strategy is about making choices. For innovation, like any business effort, resources are limited and must be deployed wisely, whether internally or externally. Even when you know what you want to achieve in the ecosystem, it can be tempting to dump a long list of underresourced projects into that bucket so you can check the box that says they are underway without some of the on-balance sheet costs. This is a false economy that in the long run can lead to wasted resources, as managers spread themselves so thin that their efforts are unrewarding.

Instead, use the four steps we have outlined to make choices. What are your top priorities? If you have projects in every zone of the frontier, which will get your time, money, and energy? Will you reallocate internal resources to the external ecosystem to meet the strategic goals and priorities you want to address? When making these decisions, you will balance short-term needs with long-term promise. Ultimately, your portfolio should feel manageable and exciting as well as justified within the current strategic priorities.

Last, find ways to explore the novelty available in the ecosystem to become exposed to what you don't know. Make space and time, however limited, for the serendipity of chance connections and novel insights that being part of an innovation ecosystem—or touring ones—can bring.

Now that you know what you want from ecosystem engagement, you can determine **who** you should work with.

Key Points from Chapter 2: What You Need from an Innovation Ecosystem

- Clarifying "what" you want from an ecosystem is needed before you engage it. This starts with creating an inventory of your current innovation projects.
- Then you need to map your existing projects to the problem/solution matrix:
  - The solution axis can use NASA's TRL framework to identify its novelty.
  - The problem axis adds a second dimension about novelty relative to your needs.
  - Projects on the matrix should also show scale (circle) and scope (color).
- The projects mapped to the problem/solution matrix provide a portfolio of your innovation efforts, which you can reconfigure to match the innovation strategy.
- This portfolio approach can help reveal where there is potential for *blind spots*—NASA's *unknown unknowns*—and *whitespace* over the horizon in your efforts;
- These efforts allow you to get specific about "what" you really need from ecosystem engagement, addressing specific zones out at the innovation horizon.
- Your organization cannot do everything, so strategy is about making choices.

Turning to chapter 3, we will now look at "who" to engage in the ecosystem.

3   Who to Engage in an Ecosystem

When GE decided to move its corporate headquarters to Boston, then-CEO Jeff Immelt explained the rationale this way: "I want some 29-year-old PhD student at MIT to punch me right in the nose and say 'all of GE's technologies are wrong and you're about to lose.'"[1]

The appeal of moving the company from rural Connecticut, where GE had been located for over one hundred years, to Boston's Seaport District was the opportunity to tap into the innovation ecosystem. Jeff noted, "Quite honestly for a big company, it makes you afraid. You're where the interference ideas are. You get more paranoid . . . and that's a good thing."[2]

Many executives feel the same palpable energy when they visit a place where innovation is flourishing. But just being present—in Boston or in any other ecosystem—is not enough. To go from being just an innovation tourist to part of the fabric of an ecosystem in a way that delivers the organizational outcomes and value you are seeking, leaders need a plan for thoughtful engagement that focuses both on what they want and who can provide it. Whom do they want to meet, understand, and learn from?

You have a range of choices. You and your team may want to connect with innovators, but you need to find the people who are working on relevant ideas, at the right phase of development, and, perhaps most importantly, interested in meeting you! Furthermore, you'll need to identify the right people within your own organization who can build fruitful relationships.

You and your teams can spend a lot of time looking for the right matches, which can be frustrating. It is also frustrating for the entrepreneurs, researchers, and venture capitalists who field random inquiries from large organizations month in and month out, without clarity on what these visitors want from them. It helps all concerned when leaders in large

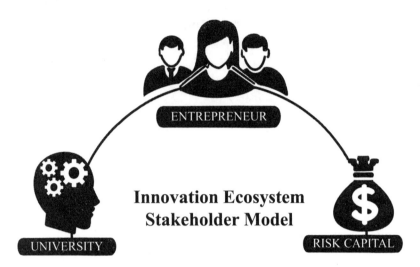

Figure 3.1
The apex 3: entrepreneur, university, and risk capital provider.

organizations identify what they want to accomplish and use that to guide who they want to talk to. This chapter explains how.

We'll start by looking in depth at the three key stakeholders at the apex of our innovation ecosystem model: entrepreneurs, universities, and risk capital providers. Today, these three, as previously described, are at the forefront of driving novelty, providing specialized resources, and experimenting. Large organization leaders are most likely to find their ecosystem innovation partners and the outcomes they seek by engaging and working among these groups. We will take a deep dive into each of these, and then we'll show you how to put the people and your innovation priorities together (see figure 3.1).

Entrepreneurs

Entrepreneurs are key stakeholders in the innovation ecosystem for the obvious reason that they are the ones increasingly taking novel ideas from inception to impact, as they found, build, and grow start-up ventures, the new enterprises in the economy.

However, finding the entrepreneurs who are working on the innovative solutions and technology that matter to you, or who understand the

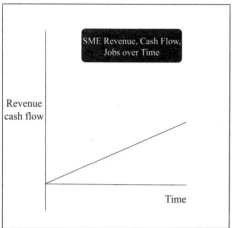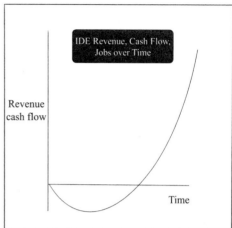

Figure 3.2
Traditional SMEs do not have the same *valley of death* as IDEs.

problems in your industry, is not easy. You are unlikely to encounter them by chance. Once you have identified a start-up with technology or an approach to your problem that seems like a good fit, you will need to dig into its business model and understand where it is in its venture-building journey. Only then will you know whether you have found the right start-up entrepreneur—and be able to make the case that a meeting, and more, will not be a waste of time for either of you.

But what type of start-up? The term is used so widely that it needs clarification. In our research, we have categorized several key types of ventures. It is worth starting, however, with a fundamental distinction between those that are likely to become small- and medium-sized enterprises (SMEs)—which tend to show a steady but slow growth path—and those in a subset of start-up ventures that we call *innovation-driven enterprises* (IDEs). The latter are the classic ventures we tend to imagine when we think about today's Silicon Valley entrepreneurs or the teams behind SpaceX or Moderna. These ventures go through significant cycles of investment and spending (known in the entrepreneurial circles as the "*valley of death*") before achieving positive cash flow (and maybe even turning a profit) (see figure 3.2).

IDEs are more likely to be aligned with your innovation strategy and goals than SMEs. Meanwhile, their need for funding for long periods while they work to reduce risk and uncertainty, and more precisely match solutions to problem, creates opportunities for the large organizations that wish to engage them.

Further Refining These IDEs

Over the last decade, we have found that a further distinction is useful within the IDE category: between more *digitally driven* IDEs (ventures whose solutions are largely based just on software) and *deep-tech* IDEs (ventures whose underlying solutions are based out on the far horizon of cutting-edge S&T, including hardware, materials, and biology).[3] This distinction is especially relevant for large organizations seeking innovation from ecosystem engagement for several reasons.

First, if the "what" that you are seeking is digital transformation in your hospital's emergency room or your back-office operations, then it is probably digital-tech IDEs (aspiring, perhaps, to become *unicorns*) who might solve your problems. When MiningCorp decided to build a *digital twin* of its mine operations, which it knew would drive much-needed productivity gains, it turned to digitally driven IDEs for help.

On the other hand, if you are seeking a next-generation therapeutic, novel satellite propulsion device or (in the case of MiningCorp) a low-energy-intensity way to refine lithium, you will need to look for deep-tech IDEs. We sometimes refer to these deep-tech ventures as *dolphins* (in recognition of their ability to remain financially submerged for long periods of time, longer than digital IDEs). They have to deploy significant amounts of capital, require highly specialized talent and other resources, and need long periods of experimentation before surfacing to solve important global challenges using breakthroughs in S&T (see figure 3.3).

Digital IDEs and deep-tech IDEs are often found in different ecosystems. Silicon Valley is most famously focused on digital-tech IDEs, an emphasis that arose from a community of entrepreneurs, first in radio communications and then in the semiconductor industry in the last century. But, of course, the ecosystem also continues to be known for its interest in related deep tech such as ventures in cutting-edge *AI* (beyond, e.g., *generative AI*).

Beyond Silicon Valley, digital IDEs have now emerged globally in ecosystems as varied as London, Berlin, Mumbai, Cape Town, and Cairo. These tend to be places with established financial expertise (London, Mumbai) and consumer-oriented businesses (Berlin), as well as places with new markets

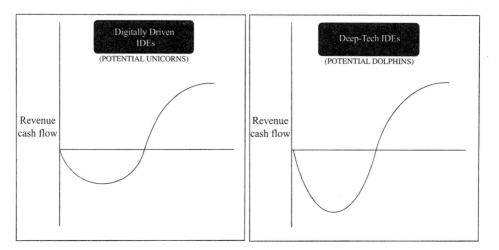

Figure 3.3
Both IDEs have an initial *valley of death*, but it is deeper for deep tech.

(across the Middle East, including Cairo and Dubai, as well as across Africa). Digital ventures can raise modest amounts of capital, prototype rapidly, and then test their software solutions on customers in a short experimentation cycle before going for additional funding rounds.

It is not surprising, then, that a global banking corporation like Barclays would have a presence in New York, London, and Mumbai to ensure that its leaders meet digital IDEs through their Rise network—a global network of fintech entrepreneurs, many of whom share space provided by Barclays in their key ecosystem locations.[4] More broadly, if you are a corporation or government department prioritizing digital transformation—especially PN zone projects and some projects in the SN zone (where you consider new business models with new customers)—then working with digitally driven IDEs in ecosystems with this expertise can amplify the impact of your portfolio.

In contrast, deep-tech IDEs have emerged across an often more distinctive set of regions and countries, according to our experience and emerging evidence—from Boston to Oxford to Copenhagen to Zurich to Singapore.[5] Additionally, these deep-tech IDEs remain much more concentrated than digital IDEs, not least because they must draw on incredibly specialized ecosystem resources that can only be found in a handful of places. Their solutions require more significant amounts of capital, longer development phases, costly scale-up, and more complex sales efforts (often with regulatory hurdles). To follow this long scale-up path to impact, deep-tech IDEs need specific technical talent and costly testing infrastructure. Moreover, they often need specialized investors who understand the challenges associated with their activities and have the patience and expertise to invest and support deep-tech ventures along their lengthy idea-to-impact journey.

If you are curious about emerging S&T, any one of the following deep-tech entrepreneurs would hold your attention with stories of their adventures:

- Bob Mumgaard, the cofounder and CEO of Commonwealth Fusion Systems (CFS), who spent over ten years at MIT developing his expertise in plasma physics. His company is developing a transformative approach to clean energy, based on building one of the world's first fusion energy systems.

- Natalya (née Brinker) Bailey, who, after getting a PhD in space propulsion at MIT, cofounded and led Accion Systems as CEO for almost a decade. Accion Systems builds propulsion systems for micro satellites.

- Lorenz Meier, CEO of Auterion, which creates operating systems for autonomous robots. Lorenz spent eight years at ETH Zurich completing his PhD in computer vision while also being an entrepreneur. He founded PX4 in 2011 and Auterion in 2018.

- Amir Basoum—whom we also met in chapter 1—is a serial entrepreneur, investing in ecosystems from Cairo to Los Angeles. He has degrees in business from the American University of Cairo as well as MIT's School of Management (where we first met him!).

- Rick, whom we also met in chapter 1, is another serial entrepreneur with expertise in the oceans working in the emerging Nova Scotia ecosystem.

All of these entrepreneurs have deep expertise. But a meeting with Bob is most useful if you are examining the energy transition and considering whether investment in CFS might provide a strong foothold in an audacious N^2 zone project—much as globally engaged Italian power company Eni decided.

An opportunity to engage with Lorenz or Natalya would be relevant if you are leading ecosystem engagement for a defense corporation like Raytheon or a government ministry, and want to add drone systems or space-based technology to your arsenal. They would also likely connect you to other innovators who have graduated from their universities, ETH and MIT, respectively, which produce a wealth of start-up ventures in deep tech.

Rick and Amir are super connectors in different communities. Those who venture to Halifax will find Rick a wealth of insight and connections to the array of maritime work occurring across that Atlantic province. Similarly, Amir is part of a densely connected group of Egyptian investors and entrepreneurs in the MENA ecosystems of Cairo and Dubai, as well as a significant group of ambitious entrepreneurs transforming healthcare in the United States and across a series of rapidly growing markets.

The places that have come to support deep-tech IDEs are ecosystems characterized by strong research universities with a focus on moving ideas out of the lab, and where there is specialization in particular technical areas. Halifax has become a center for ocean-focused IDEs, in part because it has a leading ocean engineering hub, whose expertise ranges from shipbuilding and marine autonomous systems to ocean sensing. It also has one of the world's largest natural harbors and is only an hour away from the main shipping lane across the North Atlantic between North American and Europe. Partly because of its special location, it also has unique infrastructure: home to the first naval dockyard in North America and to Canada's North Atlantic Fleet.

Across the Atlantic, as we noted earlier, Copenhagen is also becoming a strong ecosystem for deep-tech IDEs with a focus on quantum computing, in part built on its storied expertise in atomic physics at the Niels Bohr Institute. But beyond the centers of technical excellence and IDEs, this ecosystem has also built up specialized resource providers, including risk capital and experimentation infrastructure—much of it supported by the Novo Nordisk Foundation. This includes its Quantum Foundry, a facility designed to develop the fabrication, assembly, and packaging of some of the critical elements of hardware needed to build effective quantum computers.[6]

Also in Europe, we find that deep-tech IDEs are clustered in the Zurich ecosystem—including Lorenz, the founder of Auterion we introduced earlier in the chapter—in large part due to the policies and investments made by ETH Zurich. Less specialized than Copenhagen, Zurich is known for its start-up ventures at the intersection of digital and deep tech, including in robotics (e.g., Auterion), in climate technologies (including, e.g., Climeworks), and in the life sciences (especially in *medtech*).[7]

Large organizations that prioritize solutions to the complex, grand challenges in healthcare, agriculture, climate change, national security, and other socially or economically critical missions will want to connect to the specialized ecosystems supporting the deep-tech ventures most relevant to these opportunities. We will discuss exactly how to do this in chapter 4. These ecosystems can support you by filling crucial gaps in your portfolio with extremely novel solutions to your current challenges (SN zone). This is especially true for the high problem-novelty and high solution-novelty matches in the N^2 zone projects that require time and uniquely specialized resources and experiments.

Whether entrepreneurs are focused on digital innovation or deep tech, they too are on a journey that prioritizes impact and outcomes, and are doing so in the context of the ecosystem. They, too, are looking for what they need—funding and specialized resources—with their own clear sense of their road map. They also choose whom to work with. If you can help them with their journey, then engagement is more likely.

When you talk to entrepreneurs like Bob or Natalya in Boston, Rick in Nova Scotia, Lorenz in Zurich, or Amir in Cairo, consider that you might have relevant resources for them—not just money but technical expertise, customer insights, regulatory understanding, or perhaps scale-up and geopolitically savvy supply chain advice built on decades of experience. Lorenz, for example, will want to have a conversation with Kristo—a defense ministry leader—because there may be opportunities for testing and experimentation. Natalya, early in her journey, was seeking out organizational leaders in private-sector small satellite companies, advice from leaders at large corporations like Lockheed and Raytheon, as well as contacts at NASA. Bob found it helpful to engage with corporate leaders with experience in building global supply chains for massively complex products and those whose experience in audacious engineering projects set them apart. And if you offer these resources because what you want and what they need is complementary, they are more likely to talk to you. We will return to this in the next chapter on "how."

Universities

Universities are, as we have already outlined, key stakeholders in the innovation ecosystems that you wish to engage. Our university stakeholder group encompasses a wide range of institutions: globally recognized research universities, technical institutions, community colleges that produce talent for emerging industries, technical support organizations, and government (national) laboratories. These institutions focus on the earliest stages of the innovation journey, making scientific discoveries and then applying them to highly novel problems.

Universities are complex institutions, with many players, in various roles, offering multiple options for engagement. Taking research universities like MIT, Stanford, Imperial College London, ETH Zurich, Technion, or the National University of Singapore as models (and considering universities with an increasing commitment to research in their ecosystems, like King Abdullah University of Science and Technology in Saudi Arabia), we can start with the academic faculty, who are pushing the boundaries of their research fields and training the next generation of innovators in undergraduate- and graduate-level programs.

Professors in leading research universities want to innovate at the farthest horizon, not simply follow others. Supported by government or sometimes corporate funding, many of the new ideas generated in their laboratories (published in journals and often also patented) produce deeptech IDEs, often launched by former students. Scientists in government labs do similar research work (and they may train postdocs instead of students) and may, increasingly, have a similar interest in spinning out the technologies they develop, depending on their particular mandate.

Despite the large number of research professors in the world, the high-novelty research and patentable, start-up-worthy ideas come from a fraction of institutions. As you consider engaging with these productive innovators, note that while many are leaders in their respective fields, relatively few patent their ideas (or guide students) on the path to start-up ventures and becoming entrepreneurs.

In a recent study, Fiona Murray, working with her coauthor Mercedes Delgado, found that only twenty-five US universities produced more than 50 percent of the patents issued to university-based researchers and their students.[8] Moreover, half of those US patents were generated by only a small number of faculty members. You may find a similar skew in the countries and markets that you are looking at. If you are seeking novelty from universities in the innovation ecosystem, they and their students are the people to know.

Having located a potential source of university innovation, one option for a large organization is to sponsor research through an academic department or division of a research institution. In return, this investment can provide competitive advantage through gaining early insights into the results and possibly access to the talent (and a window into their plans for future spinout ventures). Direct funding of external research (with internal R&D) can play a powerful role in your portfolio, opening your eyes to your blind spots.

The relationships you build might help you to gather new talent for your organization, as well as widen your scope on a particular problem. This is why, for example, Italian energy company Eni has had a collaborative arrangement with MIT for over a decade, including supporting work in the MIT Energy Initiative and the MIT Laboratory for Innovation in Fusion Technologies (which is based in the same Plasma Science and Fusion Center (PSFC) where Bob Mumgaard, under the leadership of Professor Dennis Whyte, pioneered work on commercial-scale fusion power).[9]

The professors and students, meanwhile, often want more than just funding. Because they are interested in having an impact on the world, they will be curious about the problems that your organization can share with them on campus. Our colleague Vladimir Bulovic (who runs MIT. nano) often tells us that he can solve any problem; he just needs to know which one! (And his work on quantum LEDs and next-generation flexible solar panels rather proves the point.)

Traditional sponsored research partnerships, however, may take a long time to reach fruition. Laboratory research often focuses on solutions that are almost too novel—that will take too much time to get out of the lab or have no clear path forward. Therefore, we encourage leaders in large organizations to sometimes hone in on ideas at the university that are ready to spin out and be developed as start-up ventures if the problem they want to solve is an urgent one that can't wait. (But focus on research connections if you have an enduring interest in long-term, highly novel solutions).

At the university, you might consider building relationships with senior administrators as well as expert professional staff, such as those who run corporate relations, entrepreneurship programs, and translational research support activities. Those on campus who oversee specialized programs for corporate and government partners wishing to deeply engage with the flow of ideas will welcome your partnership.

You can also find potential ideas by engaging universities' *technology transfer offices* or *tech licensing offices* (*TTOs/TLOs*). These offices are responsible for helping to register and protect the IP that academic faculty generate at the institution. They then license patents to organizations, including start-ups or large companies that wish to use them.

Increasingly, research teams from universities are also seeking to spin out their ideas into their own deep-tech ventures: start-ups we refer to as *lab-based ventures*. In many institutions, faculty have time each week to work on outside projects and might, increasingly, use this time for a start-up (noting that they too will have to work through the TTO/TLO to secure a license to the patented ideas coming from their laboratory).

Students in these labs may work on start-ups with their faculty advisers or on their own. Bob Mumgaard, who got a PhD at MIT in applied plasma physics, is a good example. His company, CFS, is based on the research he did with faculty, including Professor Dennis Whyte, and with Eni, the Italian energy company we mentioned above (which has made several financial investments into the deep-tech venture CFS from early in its founding). One way to find these *lab-based ventures* is to identify the centers and labs that may be doing research that is relevant to you, and ask if the professors or graduates (especially postdocs) are planning to spin out their research.

Scientists in public or independent research labs are less likely to spin out themselves, in part due to the career structures of research scientists. If you work with these institutions, you will want to include people from your organization who can think about the commercial opportunities for the technologies being developed and how to bring them into the world.

Of course, universities are about more than academic professors and their research labs. As well as lab-based ventures, there are *dorm-based ventures* from students who have ideas for entrepreneurial ventures that come from outside the lab, which are another source of novel solutions. Increasingly, we find that students in MBA programs—and undergraduates—have ideas for dorm-based digital IDEs. These ideas may come from class work, independent projects, or even clubs and competitions.

Participating in programs for entrepreneurs, which we cover in the next chapter, is one of the best ways to meet the founders of these earliest-stage ventures. When you meet these entrepreneurs, it will be essential to consider whether it's their ideas you want or rather their talent, enthusiasm, and entrepreneurial attitude. And they will want to know what you have to offer them: mentoring, industry experience, or (perhaps) a window into the old way of doing things they want to challenge.

Risk Capital Providers

The third key stakeholder in the innovation ecosystem is the risk capital provider. In ecosystems and beyond, this group includes those providing capital at different stages along the journey from idea to impact, with most of that capital focused on how to support start-up ventures. These sorts of investors include private equity (PE) firms and financial institutions that issue commercial debt and an array of financing for scaling up businesses and large corporations that buy companies (often referred to as *M&As*, that is, *mergers and acquisitions*). They also include public markets that support *initial public offerings (IPOs)* of start-ups' shares, and so forth.

Because this book focuses on the earliest phases of innovation, most of these later-stage sources of funding are beyond its scope. Instead, we focus on the array of risk capital providers in the ecosystem who are actively engaged in supporting start-up ventures. These include angel investors, venture capitalists, and, increasingly, more mission-oriented and strategic investors who are adapting VC approaches to align capital with ventures that solve the problems they care about.

Let's look at these providers in this stakeholder group and their roles in more detail, focusing first on the archetypal financing of start-up ventures through funds (with some basics in the sidebar). We will then expand into the flavors of VC funds that have more recently adapted their structures to support missions and goals (the "what") well beyond simply commercial returns.

The financing of start-up ventures through private funds has evolved from its early modern historical origins to some common structures that are worth exploring. This is especially important for large organizations wishing to engage the right risk capital providers in the innovation ecosystem, as they vary in terms of sector, time frame, and the types of outcomes they seek. (In the sidebar, we set out some basics that are common to the main type of funds used to finance ventures.)

Given the focus of this book on the earliest stages of venture creation, it is worth pointing out that there are sources of "risk capital" that come before the formal, more institutionalized funds that we will detail below. For entrepreneurs seeking capital for their ventures, these sources include grants (often from the government), prizes (from competitions and accelerators), and even support from "family and friends." All of these are likely to finance your venture without seeking an equity (ownership) share that might reduce the entrepreneur's ownership of their venture.

After these (but still before formal funds) come more substantial sources of money, such as from angel investors (who tend to be high-net-worth individuals, possibly due to prior entrepreneurial successes). These early-stage risk capital providers will take a share in the venture in return for their funding and will wish to see a path to potential future stages of value (and investment), and in return will write more significant checks (of varying *ticket sizes*). This is especially so if an angel can mobilize support from other angels, perhaps in a syndicate. As the future valuation is unclear, such angel investments might be by a "Simple Agreement for Future Equity" (SAFE). This is a common successor to a traditional convertible note, both of which aim to unlock early risk capital for start-up ventures that are too early in their journey for formal investors.

Before we turn to these formal funds, it is worth looking (in the sidebar) at some basics of early-stage investment.

Financing Start-Up Ventures through Funds: Some Basics

The most common way to invest in start-up ventures is through a venture fund, a legal entity usually structured as a partnership, to deploy capital in start-ups by taking equity (ownership) in return for investment. In the case of today's VC, the partners who create the funds and then seek others' money to invest are known as *general partners* (*GPs*). The founding GPs are (hopefully) experienced investors who want to build up a team of fellow GPs to create a new fund that they can use to invest in exciting new start-up ventures. Each fund is time limited and focuses on a specific investment thesis: at the end of its time (nominally seven years but often a shorter period), the fund is expected to return profits based on its investments over that time frame.

To raise the private money for this fund, these GPs generally turn to large asset holders, which may include institutions such as university endowments, government sovereign wealth funds, national banks, and international finance funds, all with large pools of capital to invest. (These institutional investors will have a small percentage of their capital that they can allocate to nonpublic, *alternative asset* classes, such as investments in PE, VC, and hedge funds.) These partners, known as *limited partners* (*LPs*), provide most of the money for the fund and therefore expect to receive (most of the) benefits for those on whose behalf they are allocating capital. These benefits from VC funds usually come when the GPs *exit* their equity positions in the successful ventures they have chosen and close the fund.

As a rule, GPs make equity investments in a large number of start-up ventures (known as their *portfolio*) to manage the risk of taking an equity stake in early-stage start-ups. They will often designate one of their partners to sit on the board of the start-up ventures, which helps ensure that the entrepreneurs focus on their specific goals and strategies of reducing the considerable risks they face in taking their idea on the inception-to-impact journey. The GPs will often look to set up new funds, even while the first one is underway, so that they can spread their risk over time and market conditions. As GPs charge 2 percent fees annually on their money under management, no matter how those investments are doing, they have an incentive to be running several funds at once, as the overall volume of money leads to higher annual fees.

Most VC funds, and indeed most GPs, specialize their investing in start-ups in specific sectors and in different stages on the journey to truly understand the challenges and opportunities of those sectors. For example, Katie Rae, the founding GP at the Engine Ventures (a fund based close to MIT in Kendall Square), focuses on deep-tech solutions and was an early investor in CFS.[10] Other partners in the Engine Ventures work on industrial systems or life sciences. In Europe, Klaus Hommels is the longtime founder and GP of Lakestar Ventures (based in London, Berlin, and Zurich) and focuses more on digital tech, with investments including Revolut (the fintech based in London) and Spotify (the music service from Sweden) but with a growing interest in deep tech including ventures emerging from European universities.

GPs like Katie and Klaus make choices around their funds' geographic scope (i.e., which innovation ecosystems), their chosen sectors, and their focus (starting with problems, e.g., healthcare, climate, or finance challenges) or solutions (e.g., life sciences, crypto, or energy technologies). They also choose between nearer-term digital tech and longer-term deep tech, as well as their preferred investment stage (i.e., early stage with ventures that require funds to prototype and pilot, or later-stage investing for scaling and expansion). This allows GP teams to build specialized knowledge and relationships with start-up entrepreneurs and their teams. This expertise is especially important in early-stage investing, when risks are high and ideas are far out on the innovation horizon.

Every fund has a defined lifetime—often ten years for a standard VC fund, but operationally they are typically more like seven—at the end of which the GPs must return the original capital to the LPs, plus any additional returns (minus the GPs' 20 percent share) that have been generated from the fund's investments. This assumes that the fund has made a return by unlocking the investments' value through a *liquidity event*—also known as an *exit*—that lets investors get their returns, for example, by the start-up venture listing on a public market or being acquired by a large corporation (or follow-on private fund). Successful GPs will raise multiple funds in sequence, leveraging their success with their initial funds, so they always have capital for them to invest.

VC Funds

VC is a particular sort of risk capital that, over the years, has been adapted to suit the needs of early-stage entrepreneurial ventures (mainly IDEs). It was founded in Boston in the late 1940s, grew up in the 1950s, and has accompanied, and been a crucial driver of, the formation of innovation ecosystems. The focus of VCs on investing in early-stage IDEs—high-growth potential ventures in deep tech and then mostly digital tech—makes them especially interesting as a stakeholder to engage when it comes to connecting to interesting, high-potential start-ups that might meet your strategic goals.

You can learn about the role that VCs play in ecosystems that matter to you—and work out whether you can gain insights from them—by understanding their investment thesis and portfolio of companies. This shows you whether a fund aligns with your innovation priorities; the fund strategy shapes the flow of novel ideas and talented people the VC is likely to see and thus the types of ideas and people they might be willing to discuss with you. For example, Lakestar, one of several early investors in Lorenz Meier's Auterion, is active across a range of the most vibrant European ecosystems and refers to the approach as being "European heart. Global mind."[11] The company invests from offices in Berlin, Zurich, and London—across stages from seed to growth—and their portfolio includes an emphasis on vertical software (digitization of established industries) and more recently deep tech and some healthcare.

VC fund strategies generally have several dimensions that you will also need considered in answering the "what" of your innovation portfolio:

- They define the phase of venture they are interested in (e.g., pre-seed, seed, then Series A, B, C, etc.), which corresponds to how far along the idea-to-impact journey the venture is and thus how much novelty and risk they are managing.
- They are often creatures of their home ecosystem, with a narrow geographic focus, though large VC firms may have offices in multiple ecosystems.
- They define their strategies by markets and therefore support solutions that solve problems for that set of customers or technologies. They also tend to invest in solutions in specific sectors such as life sciences, finance, AI, or cybersecurity.

The majority of VC funds have come to focus on consumer markets, such as software, fintech, and insurance, though historically VC-style funds and structures were developed to invest in silicon semiconductors and the early generations of computer hardware. (A good example, sometimes referred to as "the forerunner to modern VC," was American Research and Development (ARD), described by Sebastian Mallaby in his book *The Power Law*.)[12] Building on those foundations, many VCs in Silicon Valley discovered that the relatively limited resource needs and short experimental cycles of digital technology were more viable, as investments could be made in the first years of the fund and deliver returns (hopefully at the "10x" scale) early, before the fund's official end.

VC firms do not cover every zone of the innovation portfolio where you might have a gap to fill or opportunity to pursue. In fact, today's VC industry has been criticized for focusing their investments largely on a few, quick-return digital sectors, meaning that you might miss some important novel ideas and exciting entrepreneurial talent if you only work through VCs in your innovation ecosystem interactions.

The traditional structure of VC funds, with their limited time horizon, is viewed by some as the reason for underinvestment in the sorts of ventures that might produce a COVID-19 vaccine, a new quantum computer for better encryption, or a novel approach to commercial-scale fusion energy.[13] Nonetheless, other funds have specialized in investments in the life sciences, especially in San Francisco, San Diego, Boston, and the UK (around Oxford and Cambridge). The well-structured stages, shaped by clear regulatory pathways, have made it possible to get returns over a ten-year period, especially when the biotech ventures enter into partnerships with (or are acquired by) large corporates (particularly pharmaceutical companies).

Some funds focus on new entrepreneurs or new, emerging innovation ecosystems, and so they have the potential to connect you to other sources of novelty and talent:

- Future Africa is a fund based in Nigeria and Kenya, making investments in digital-tech IDEs scaling across Africa's fast-growing markets.[14]
- FirstCheck Africa specifically focuses on funding female entrepreneurs across the continent.
- Unshackled Ventures, which invests in firms started by immigrants to the United States, is based in San Francisco.

If you are interested in problems or solutions with a longer horizon, especially in deep-tech sectors beyond the life sciences, you may have to look harder for VC funds with priorities that match your own. That said, some of the largest and best-known funds have expanded into deep tech. These include A16Z, which now invests in the life sciences (largely in Silicon Valley), as well as fintech (in London) and defense and security (through its American Dynamism fund).[15] Yet others, including Lakestar and LocalGlobe in Europe, have a mix of digital- and deep-tech investments. Closer to home in Kendall Square, Engine Ventures has a portfolio entirely composed of deep-tech start-up ventures, dealing with the extended timelines of these investments by taking the unusual step of extending the fund life from seven to twelve years.

Mission-Oriented Funds

If you are looking for specific ideas, and especially start-up ventures in areas that are of global significance beyond simply their market potential, sooner or later you will likely run into a range of so-called *mission-oriented* or impact venture funds. These have adapted aspects of the original *risk capital* and now VC approaches to crowd capital into areas that are otherwise underserved or address broader economic, societal or *dual-use* problems. If these categories are high on your "what" list of priorities, you will likely want to engage with these newer sorts of investors. And it may be easy to find common ground due to their focus on a critical mission you both care about.

As with traditional venture funds, understanding the problems or solutions they invest in will help you determine whether one of these mission-oriented VCs is a good match to your priorities. It is also worth understanding the degree to which these funds aim to make expected rates of market returns, have a specific investment focus connected to mission areas, and have a longer-time horizon for providing returns to allow the sorts of (often deep-tech) ventures they invest in to bear fruit.

Like traditional VC funds, some mission-oriented funds focus on new problems, especially where markets are more complex and emerging, including the following:

- In climate, Breakthrough Energy Ventures (BEV), started by Microsoft founder Bill Gates and his billionaire colleagues, has a large portfolio of investments in the US and Europe. These focus on ventures with massive climate mitigation potential in areas where the carbon removal market is still poorly structured, leading to underinvestment in climate solutions.

- In healthcare, various models have emerged. Funds like Hopelab Ventures is a mission-aligned social impact investor with a fund focused on mental health challenges. Alternatively, based within its foundation, J&J Impact Ventures is a fund focused on addressing health equity.

- Defense and security-focused funds, such as the American Technological Innovation Fund, focus on companies that need long-term capital and expertise to help them through multiyear government contracts. Another example is In-Q-Tel, a US government–created nonprofit fund that supports ventures (often with *dual-use* strategies) whose solutions target the mission needs of the intelligence community.

Regardless of the debate over the role of traditional VCs in the innovation economy, you will need to judge whether their priorities can usefully address the "what" that you have defined as your priority. And if you have found useful VCs or other risk capital providers to engage, then now is the time to consider how to build a trusted relationship.

However, this is challenging: VCs do not commonly build formal relationships with large corporates unless the latter invest in the fund as an LP. A more common alternative, as we will explore in the next chapter, is when organizations have their own "strategic" venture fund, such as a corporate venture fund or a government venture fund. These funds will then have a natural way to interact through co-investment in start-ups of mutual interest—similar to how Eni engaged with CFS alongside Engine Ventures, or how Boeing's HorizonX venture fund, along with other, more traditional VCs, invested in Natalya Bailey's Accion Systems. (We'll talk in more detail about this approach in the next chapter.) This lays the foundation for deeper relationships, sharing of opportunities, and so on. But otherwise, it is worth understanding how to engage with VCs and the ways in which you, as a corporate or government stakeholder, can consider how to connect and, importantly, recall what you bring to the table for entrepreneurs (whom VCs, after all, want to be extremely successful)!

Put the People and Priorities Together

Now that you know the stakeholders and their roles in the ecosystem, let's look at a way to identify who you want to work with and where to find them. It is time to make sense of the wealth of people you are likely to meet when you walk the streets of the innovation ecosystem and determine who the best people are in your organization to engage with them. As we've said, if you know what you want to accomplish from your ecosystem engagement, you will be able to figure out whom you need to meet. The people you meet will appreciate your clarity and focus and find it a refreshing change from the innovation tourism that they will often encounter. It will be more efficient and more effective for you as well.

The PN Zone: Mostly Digitally Focused Entrepreneurs

If you prioritize the PN zone (existing solutions to novel problems), then entrepreneurs—especially those with a digital focus (and unicorn aspirations)—will be essential to your efforts. You will often be seeking digitally driven IDEs whose talent and expertise in the digital domain surpass that of your organization. These companies will be developing solutions. They may be looking for customer insights or a testbed "in the wild" for their solution. For example, if you are working at a leading medical center, you might want to meet an entrepreneur like Amir Basoum so that your organization can connect with and learn from Vezeeta's experience in bringing digital health efficiencies to emerging markets.

In this zone, you will be pursuing solutions for new customers, new needs, or new use cases. Therefore, leaders in your customer-facing units, or your product managers, should probably build these relationships. Entrepreneurs like Amir may also hope to learn from and partner with you. This is especially true if you are engaged with an emerging ecosystem such as Cairo, Lagos, or Mumbai, where entrepreneurs might have fewer opportunities to partner with large companies or government agencies.

The SN Zone: Universities, Deep-Tech Entrepreneurs, and Some Risk Capital Providers

If you are prioritizing the SN zone—filling a gap in your portfolio with novel solutions to existing problems, or seeking more sources of novelty and new talent—then universities can be powerful sources of partnership, insight, and inspiration. Closely related will be start-ups that spin out from the university labs, often enterprises with a more deep-tech focus, supported by some risk capital providers.

If you are seeking early-stage, very novel solutions, you can find the world-leading experts who themselves are looking for insights into the problems that might be solved. You will likely have fewer locations to choose from (and fewer stakeholders as well), as the frontiers of novel S&T are not evenly distributed and are highly specialized. But you might find that some smaller universities or smaller ecosystems have extraordinary pockets of deep-tech expertise (like Dalhousie in Halifax for ocean S&T, the University of Copenhagen for quantum, and ETH Zurich for robotics) and are starting to build IDE spinouts. You can learn about spinouts from the TLO and from the university labs themselves, but for companies at a later stage, insights might come from the risk capital providers who support some deep tech like Klaus, whom we discussed earlier, and more specialized funds like Engine Ventures, where Katie and her team, invest in deep-tech ventures coming out of MIT, Harvard, and universities across the US.

While it is hard to determine who to send to gain insights for SN zone opportunities, we have found it useful when large organizations send experienced technical experts to universities to engage with faculty and students, and even when those same individuals talk to investors (as you can be useful and help investors appreciate the technical opportunities, risks, and challenges of the novel solutions they are generating). Your experienced engineers are also valuable in conversations with deep-tech entrepreneurs: MIT colleagues in the fusion center (and their CFS colleagues) learned from conversations with engineering leaders in corporations like Eni, which have deep experience building complex and precise engineering systems at scale.

The N^2 Zone: Risk Capital Providers and Deep-Tech Entrepreneurs

Finally, if your interests lie in highly novel solutions to highly novel problems, you might find a meeting of minds and priorities with some of the more specialized, mission-oriented risk capital providers and the types of entrepreneurs they support (usually of the deep-tech dolphin variety), who are exploring the same part of the innovation horizon and with a shared mission and purpose.

They will likely appreciate your potential to scale supply chains and provide financing that enables eventual solutions to be deployed at global scale, and your willingness to explore how new regulatory pathways might also need to be forged to ensure that these novel ideas are brought to scale.

In the N^2 zone especially, the value of long-term ecosystem engagement with start-up entrepreneurs and their investors (and the universities they emerge from) is likely to be especially valuable, as the risks and uncertainty associated with many N^2 zone projects mean that their final outcomes are hard to predict. Additionally, there are likely to be significant bumps in the road to success, where your ongoing expertise and engagement might be most valued. This is certainly true for entrepreneurs in quantum computing from Vancouver and Boston to London and Copenhagen. They value interactions with government leaders who have insights into regulatory pathways and government partnerships (and contracts). They will also value talking to you if you bring large corporate expertise in engineering at scale, in partnerships, and in supply chains.

Where to Find the Right People

Once you know whom you should be engaging, the next step is to clarify where in the world—in which ecosystem—you will find these people. A mature, globally renowned ecosystem may be the right place, but it may also be crowded. By all means plan a trip to Silicon Valley or Singapore for inspiration. Yet consider that an emerging ecosystem may fit your needs closer to home, and the people in them may have more time for you because there is less competition for their attention.[16]

Ultimately, four factors influence where most organizations choose to engage.

Source of Opportunities

Ideally, organizations will choose their ecosystem locations based on opportunities: which innovation ecosystem has the best set of opportunities (across the zones) to support their priorities, like BAE Systems in Boston. This idealized starting point will be balanced with your organization's location. Some organizations are lucky enough to already operate in mature, famous innovation ecosystems. For them, the primary choice of location may be straightforward. Others will be more like GE or like some of the major pharmaceutical companies that were close to Boston (in Connecticut and New Jersey) but not embedded within relevant innovation ecosystems. They also have a somewhat easy choice, answering the question "who" with the answer almost "in their own back yard"! For example, the insurance company MassMutual is headquartered in Springfield, Massachusetts, just one hundred miles west of the Greater Boston ecosystem.

For other organizations already located in emerging ecosystems that may not be globally renowned, there may be fewer entrepreneurs and risk capital providers. However, they might still offer the novelty and specialized resources you need, in which case opportunities and priorities are already aligned—our colleagues in Cairo and Lagos are a case in point. A focus on smaller or emerging ecosystems may be especially worthwhile if you want to work with digitally focused IDEs, as communications technologies that enable remote working have accelerated the creation of digital start-ups around the world. You might not need to trek to Silicon Valley. Similarly, if a local emerging ecosystem has the sort of deep-tech focus you need, then you are likely to find the support you need and, in turn, support the ecosystem's goals.

Resource Constraints

As you consider locations that maximize opportunities for novelty, resources, and experimentation, resource constraints come into play. Working with partners outside the usual geographic footprint of your organization can be costly, not only in terms of travel or set-up costs but also because of the challenge of competing for attention in a busy, globally renowned ecosystem.

Engaging with a local ecosystem (whether established or emerging) is less costly than an exciting distant one, and it may be more resource efficient as long as it meets your needs or has the potential to do so (with some investment and attention).

Local Obligations

Many public sector organizations (and some state-owned corporate enterprises) are also required to primarily engage with ecosystems in their own country or region. The same may be true of foundations whose charitable mission may be constrained by geographic boundaries.

Even a large corporation, if it has a role as a national champion, might face some constraints to the geographic scope of its ecosystem engagement. For example, leaders at Aramco in eastern Saudi Arabia had to integrate their local and national obligations to the country with their wider role in economic prosperity into their innovation priorities. As a result, for these organizations, the geographic choice will be a simple one: they will start with their local innovation ecosystem (even if it may not be the best suited to support their priorities). For those like Belinda or Kristo, their home city (and certainly their home country) may be the starting point for their interactions. That said, they may choose one or two others based on existing governmentally oriented alliances. For large corporations like Eni and Aramco, local engagement might also be balanced with a global choice—for both corporates, Greater Boston has been one such.

The Right Number of Locations

Finally, organizations may consider whether or not what they need from an ecosystem is sufficiently broad in scope to require engaging with multiple ecosystems. Developing a sense of whether your organization can afford to engage with one innovation ecosystem, or may have the resources to interact with a small handful of places, is an important starting point in choosing where to engage. It is easier, in our experience, to connect deeply to one or two places than spreading your resources too thinly and thus receiving little in return.

The multi-ecosystem approach has been pursued by some, typically large, organizations. For example, Barclays operates across three locations—London, New York, and Mumbai—which allows it to tap into solutions that address different customer needs and are designed for distinctive regulatory environments. Philips Healthcare is active in Eindhoven (its Dutch headquarters), but also Greater Boston and Bangalore, where demographic differences offer opportunities to understand the medical needs of populations on three continents, as well as different medical cultures and healthcare systems. J&J, working on the healthcare side, has innovation teams working in four hubs around the world, and it has smaller-scale incubation and accelerator programs in eleven locations.

A multi-ecosystem approach can, however, be complex and costly given the level of management and coordination it entails. But it offers some organizations the chance to tap into an extraordinarily varied and diverse set of opportunities. They can compare and learn from what is happening in different locations, potentially creating synergies among their efforts by offering entrepreneurs the chance to connect with counterparts in other ecosystems. Uber, for instance, has an advanced technologies group with offices in San Francisco (close to headquarters) and Pittsburgh (where Carnegie Mellon University has a world-leading research group focused on autonomy), as well as in India.

When you answer the strategic question about "who" in an ecosystem you need to engage for your innovation effort, and you figure out where these people are located, you will also want to consider whether you also need to locate some staff in those ecosystems.

Key Points from Chapter 3: Who to Engage in an Ecosystem

Having determined "what" your large organization needs from an ecosystem, it is important to decide "who" to engage to most effectively help you with that.

- Place-based innovation ecosystems comprise five stakeholders, but the three at the apex are the ones most likely to be of interest to large organizations, as follows:
    - **Entrepreneurs**—whose start-ups are at the IDE end of the spectrum (rather than the majority that will be SMEs)—might focus on digital tech (often with a *unicorn* aspiration) or on deep tech (drawing on emerging S&T as *dolphins*)
    - **Universities**, and similar research organizations, that are likely to do relevant research and produce solutions (either as patents or spinout ventures)
    - **Risk capital** providers, including institutionalized VC as well as those seeking more strategic (rather than financial) returns, including on impact
- Bringing together the "what" and "who," it is important to refine exactly which type of stakeholders can help you with your innovation challenge by zone.
- Having identified a right "who" within these stakeholder categories, it is key to be strategic about finding them, either in local or world-class ecosystems.
- Shaping your search for these people are four factors: the source of opportunities, your resource constraints and local obligations, and the right number of locations.

Turning to chapter 4, we will now look at "how" to engage an ecosystem.

4 How to Engage in an Ecosystem

At this point in the development of your ecosystem engagement strategy, you will have determined the "what" and the "who": the strategic priorities you have for your external innovation ecosystem interactions and the ways in which these are complementary to, but differentiated from, your internal innovation system activities. On the "who," you will also have done a deep dive into whom you wish to engage in the ecosystem. These are the people outside your organization whose work and ideas will support your priorities. Additionally, you will identify those from within your organization who might most effectively lead your engagements. This leaves you with one final, essential question: *how* exactly are you going to engage the ecosystem?

Faced with this question, many leaders declare that it's time to "get started!" Sometimes, after a series of conversations with entrepreneurs and investors in several ecosystems, or maybe just with relatives over dinner, they tell their organization to run a hackathon. Or a bootcamp. Or an innovation workshop!

Others will have read about the ambitious Defense Advanced Research Projects Agency (DARPA) Grand Challenge for autonomous vehicles and the more recent Subterranean Challenge competition to map the seabed—all inspired, in part, by the 1714 Longitude Prize (to help navigators accurately determine their longitude)—and decide a challenge or prize competition must be the answer. Or, spurred by a *New York Times* story about innovation that referenced Y Combinator and *demo days*, they decide to build an *accelerator*.[1]

Perhaps they become inspired to hold a splashy one-off event. Or they open a glamorous office in their favorite innovation ecosystem, purchase some orange "innovation-ready" sofas, and hang out a sign declaring that their "innovation lab" is open for visitors.

Occasionally, if an organization is fortunate, these choices might lead to some productive outcomes. More often, they fall flat. They deliver something of interest but not the innovation that was the clearly defined priority. And yet they will have taken time, resources, and attention.

Nothing may happen at all. Corporate leaders complain that they have "arrived" in the ecosystem, but no one seems to have noticed. A newly opened space sees no traffic; a press release gets no attention. What they haven't realized is that things like opening up an office or holding a party in an ecosystem are not a good answer to the "how" question. Entrepreneurs and innovators are busy. They don't notice activities that don't align with their own innovation process and objectives, or with people who do not clearly share their vision and commitment.

A solid understanding of the innovation processes at work in the ecosystem can help you avoid these missteps. To start, we will lay out the sequence of *innovation cycles* that are the hallmark of most innovation processes in "the wild" of the ecosystem. We will then outline the different programs that have arisen to support each of these cycles—the hackathons, prize competitions, accelerators, and options for scaling. These are often the most effective programs for large organizations to engage with to meet start-ups, university labs, or risk capital providers.

We then turn inward and show you how to assess your internal innovation process to ensure you have mechanisms in place to "pull through" and integrate the novel ideas and talented people you identify and support externally at every stage and cycle in their own journey. Finally, we show you how to put these two pieces together and help ensure successful outcomes that meet your priorities.

This last part is essential: without working out how your external ecosystem engagement efforts and internal innovation system connect, good ideas will get lost. You will never get all the impact that they promise, your efforts will not be valued, and, often, they will then be shuttered or have a significant reduction in funding.

The earliest days of the Defense Innovation Unit (DIU) in Boston illustrate the sort of unintended outcomes that happen when teams do not fully appreciate the innovation processes at work in the ecosystem and how to effectively connect to them. DIU, formed in 2015, was one of a series of three Pentagon outposts in innovation ecosystems—the others being the original one in Silicon Valley, and then a later one in Austin, Texas. The unit was tasked with finding start-ups with products that might be adapted to the needs of the military, quickly purchased, and rapidly deployed.[2]

However, this DIU unit (close to our own offices in Greater Boston) had one small but important challenge. The space it had selected, though in a desirable location, was just outside of the daily flow of Kendall Square. It was beautiful once you were inside, but because of security needs, getting in was an arduous process. As a result, the unit's early events, where it hoped to meet, inspire, and engage entrepreneurs who might have potential solutions to their hard to solve problems, fell flat. For early-stage entrepreneurs who were simply curious about DIU, it was just too much hassle to take the time with all the previsit paperwork requirements to participate in a new and relatively untested activity, however important it might be to the nation. If the meeting was about a large-scale contract or opportunity to test out ideas in partnership, then they would go the extra mile. But so early in the innovation cycle, it was just too complex and delivered too little value.

The head of the Boston unit—then-Colonel Michael McGinley (aka "Col. Mike")—started over. His DIU team reconfigured the space to make part of it more accessible with less bureaucracy. They also designed programs to bring in military reservists, currently attending local public policy and business schools, to map out who the interesting local start-ups might be and whether their ideas might be a good match to some of the challenges posed by frontline commands, so that they could be more targeting in their outreach. The team started organizing events to share the Pentagon's mission challenges, and interest in DIU grew, with the community of innovators increasingly excited about the novel problems that the unit was hoping to solve, and the opportunity to work on an important national security mission. Within a few months, the space and the unit came to life, and the much hoped-for strategic benefits started to follow.

Our rather methodical approach to the "how" of ecosystem engagement isn't sexy or splashy. But if you step back and follow our simple lessons, they will help you understand the innovation cycles of the entrepreneurs, innovators, and their investors, thus helping you determine where in the innovation process you want to intervene. They will also help you identify the right ecosystem programs from the wealth of existing activities, allowing you to select those that best meet your needs and engage with as many of the right innovators and entrepreneurs as possible to accomplish your priorities.

And last, as we will illustrate when we return to your own internal innovation process, our approach will ensure that you can more effectively bring novel ideas back into your own organizations, whether they are large government agencies like the Pentagon where Mike McGinley was operating or a large corporation like DSM Venturing, where Pieter Wolters was a leader.

Innovation Cycles in the External Ecosystem

Innovation *cycles*—the phases of funding, experimentation, and learning that start-up entrepreneurs go through in the wild of an ecosystem—are analogous to the often more structured innovation *stages* within a large organization's pipeline. Even though an ecosystem might seem chaotic and messy—an image that its entrepreneurs, researchers, and investors often relish—in fact systematic and staged choices help them to experiment, demonstrate the value of their ideas, and reduce risks.

In each innovation cycle, teams gather the specialized resources they need and carefully experiment. At the end of each cycle, they (and their investors) evaluate what they have learned, which assumptions were confirmed or disproved, whether they have reached a critical milestone, and then which experiment (and with how much money) to pursue next to create value. Or they might stop the project if the results are poor and those involved believe their time is better spent elsewhere.

These experiments, at whatever cycle, are most effective when they are designed to reduce the most important risks associated with both the problem and the solution that lie at the core of the idea at its current stage of development—whether that is a question about, for example, customer adoption (the problem to solve) or technical scale-up (the solution being developed). Entrepreneurs will use a range of different experimentation methods, choosing ones that are appropriate for whatever cycle they are in and whatever risk they feel is most essential to evaluate. These include methods that, as an innovation leader in large organizations, you might be familiar with from popular books or perhaps because you have started to use them in pockets of activity within your organization: *lean start-up, business model canvas, design thinking,* and *minimum viable products* among them.[3] To these customer- and market-oriented activities, it is important to add the more traditional technical experiments at lab or bench scale, up to later pilots and demonstrations. These are all methods for rapid learning that entrepreneurs deploy at each cycle in their journey toward scaling and successful growth to reduce (or "retire") the risks that their experiments were designed to test.

At the end of each stage, armed with their experimental evidence and to close the "cycle," the innovators, entrepreneurs, and their investors (or other resource providers) must evaluate the results of the experiment and decide on whether to proceed to the next, depending on the results of the prior one. In instances when the experiment has gone according to plan, the team may well evaluate the evidence and conclude that risks have been reduced, positive lessons have been learned about the idea, and a milestone has been reached. And so, with this positive evaluation, the team will continue to the next larger and more resource-intensive cycle. Alternatively, of course, the experiment in an innovation cycle may generate information that the solution is not what the problem owners hoped for: it might be too slow, too costly, or too limited in its performance. If the desired outcome has not transpired, the entrepreneurs (and investors) may adapt the experiment. Or, they may change path (a shift sometimes referred to as a *pivot*). And, in some cases, the project must be stopped completely (see figure 4.1).

Cycles of experimentation and evaluation are repeated, as successful projects gain growing positive evidence and interest, while other, less successful, ones are stopped. For simplicity's sake, we label these repeated cycles simply as 1, 2, 3, and 4. For teams you will meet in the ecosystem (rather than inside a large organization), even if they have created valuable

Figure 4.1
Innovation "cycles" that downselect ideas and resource-up those that are successful.

evidence in their experiments, they must still look for additional resources—specialized people, money, and infrastructure—to move to the next cycle and pursue the next set of experiments. This might be from those already engaged or from new investors whose interests and risk tolerance are more suited to later stages of investing. In later cycles, these are more closely associated with the start of formal funding stages, so later ventures will often be asked what funding *round* they have completed—for example, pre-seed, seed, and then Series A, B, and so on. That is where early financing rounds overlap with later innovation cycles.

All of the entrepreneurs you have met in the course of reading this book will have been through these cycles, and most—including Bob Mumgaard and Natalya Bailey—will have cycles underway, hoping to reach critical milestones in their journey to create significant value and wider impact. Innovation leaders in large organizations must be aware of the resource (and time) needs of such start-up entrepreneurs so that they have realistic expectations about what it will take, and how long it will take, to achieve the novelty they are seeking. To this end, understanding the cycle of the start-up is a key "shortcut" to determining whether a particular entrepreneurial venture is at a stage in its idea-to-impact journey that aligns with your organizational priorities.

As a rule, as we illustrate in figure 4.2, the activities in each cycle vary, with early discovery ones focused on *exploring* and *validating* the essential problem/solution match. Later delivery cycles then shift to *accelerating* and *scaling* the idea by reducing both the solution risk (including the ability to produce the solution at scale) and the problem risk (including understanding the regulatory context for customer adoption, etc.).

A project will start with small amounts of resources to explore assumptions about the problem and solution, and then define the core idea of the venture. Over time, if it progresses through each cycle, it will gather more—and more specialized—resources to power bigger, more costly experiments and to test assumptions at an increasing scale, with a focus on accelerating activities and scaling growth. Indeed, teams leading entrepreneurial ventures are now advised to begin with fast, low-cost experiments, often before taking any significant sources of external risk capital. Such early funding could come from a grant program, perhaps from within a university, from friends and family, or from some of the investors we met in chapter 3 who

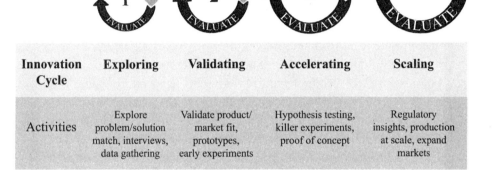

Innovation Cycle	Exploring	Validating	Accelerating	Scaling
Activities	Explore problem/solution match, interviews, data gathering	Validate product/ market fit, prototypes, early experiments	Hypothesis testing, killer experiments, proof of concept	Regulatory insights, production at scale, expand markets

Figure 4.2
Mapping entrepreneurial activities to the innovation "cycles."

specialize in very early-stage companies (including angels and early-stage VCs) or those with expertise in later stages of growth (VCs sometimes referred to as growth funds). Later, outside equity capital will be invested in a series of funding *rounds*, which effectively match the later experimental cycles of learning and de-risking. Venture start-ups use this range of funds to expand their team, build relevant expertise, and gather other resources so that they can experiment more effectively.

The length of these cycles—and the amount of support required—can vary depending on whether the start-ups are principally digital or more focused on deep tech. It is worth understanding some of the differences in the innovation cycles of digital- versus deep-tech ventures, as their stages are different in length and size in ways that mean that your ecosystem interactions with them will be quite distinctive.

Deep-tech ventures may need to build entirely new hardware and use expensive, specialized facilities that they have to access or perhaps even have to invent: in these cases, even an early cycle may take years and millions. The teams in these sorts of ventures start with low-TRL ideas: a published theory, an experiment at the lab bench. They then move to a larger-scale lab and then into a pilot demonstration. Only if this has proven effective will they move to the much more costly activity of building the solution at full commercial scale.

A case in point is CFS, the fusion energy company led by Bob Mumgaard. The company aims to build a fusion energy reactor at a commercial scale that is robust, reliable, and "net positive" (i.e., produces more energy than it consumes creating the fusion reaction). An early experimental cycle called for the team to engineer an entirely new type of magnetic material capable of holding plasma (i.e., the source of the tremendous power of a fusion reactor). Given the technical risks, with temperatures comparable to those of the sun, it was uncertain whether the material could be created at scale and engineered into a working large magnet. Only when they succeeded (which they did, after an experimental cycle lasting around two years) were they able to move on to the next innovation cycle and the next experiment: building their entire fusion reactor system at a 50 percent scale in the pilot phase.

Digital companies in an early cycle look dramatically different (and cheaper!): they may just need to hire programmers to code an online platform and so may be able to complete an early cycle in a few months. Overall, their cycles of software development can be quick, and they need fewer resources than deep-tech ventures. For example, a company like Vezeeta could test and adapt its software much more swiftly than CFS could test its hardware—in a matter of months compared to years and with 100x less capital. Of course, it's not enough for the software to work (or hardware, for that matter). Entrepreneurs also need cycles to test whether their solutions are good matches to the problem they are trying to solve (a precursor form of *product/market fit*). They will experiment to learn precise customer needs and the cost of customer acquisition.

The Vezeeta team needed to understand whether patients and their physicians would be willing to work with an online scheduling and meeting system: they trialed this in their hometown of Cairo, a market not used to digital healthcare delivery. In one cycle, the team tested mock-ups of their doctors' selecting and scheduling application, starting with screen wireframes of the proposed application, thus *validating* the product. At the next cycle, they needed to build the entire backend for the scheduling system to test the cost of adoption by the medical providers themselves, subsequently shifting focus to accelerate the company by working with a large number of patients.

Of course, no projects happen in a vacuum. Innovation ecosystems are competitive places, just like ones in nature. Start-ups might proceed rapidly, be forced to adapt, or rapidly die. For the average SME, according to the US Bureau of Labor, around 50 percent of those founded have failed within the first five years. Of these, the fraction of SMEs that are actually IDEs, and get venture funding, is only about 0.05 percent. And even these die at a high rate: only about 40 percent of start-ups with seed-stage funding make it to Series A. And of those, only about 65 percent will make it through the Darwinian process of *downselection* from Series A to B.[4] It is thus truly "survival of the fittest," and something similar should be true within a large organization's internal pipeline.

In the ecosystem, the downselection process might seem less organized and structured than that inside your organization, in part because it involves a wider range of players. Within the ecosystem, the trajectories of an idea that can be pursued by a team are more diverse, informed by founders selecting the direction to develop, entrepreneurial talent deciding which venture to join and for how long, and many different investors deciding on committing capital (or not). There is not just one single *stage gate* to pass through but a whole series of people deciding to accept or reject an entrepreneur's proposal for the next cycle and options for funding each cycle. As a result, people direct and redirect themselves, as well as resources and attention, to whatever projects are most effective. The surviving ideas then get better resourced.

Internally, with your *pipeline* equivalent to the ecosystem's cycles, you will wish to think about the lessons you can draw from these external practices (see figure 4.3). On the one hand, your internal multistage processes in the organization often apply similar decision points—for example, *stage gates*—and filters to all ideas, but with judgments made by the same set of internal people, often in the same room, with the same template and same questions. On the other hand, it is sometimes difficult within large organizations to achieve the diversity of opinions, risk-taking, and the rigor of investor expectations, as well as speed of the ecosystem. However, paying attention to how start-ups thrive or fail in the external ecosystem can help shape your internal system. Equally important, it can shape your decision about "how"—that is, when and in which ways—to link the external innovation cycles in the ecosystem to the stages in your internal innovation system.

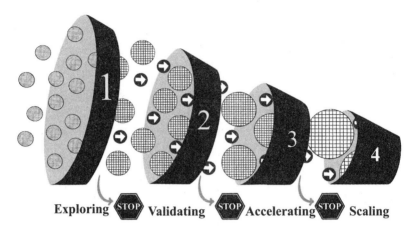

Figure 4.3
The four-stage internal "pipeline" for downselecting ideas.

Programs in the Innovation Ecosystem

Innovation ecosystems have generated a large number of programs that support the exploring and validating cycles of venture formation as well as the accelerating and scaling cycles. These programs—which include well-known activities like hackathons and accelerators—shape the selection and support, and the deselection and demise, of new entrepreneurial ventures. Innovation ecosystems are no longer entirely unstructured, with entrepreneurs and their investors competing and matching in a sea of ideas and resources. Instead, these programs have evolved to provide structure to innovation cycles to help some entrepreneurs quickly and efficiently access the specialized advice, innovative talent, and other resources that they need rather than leave them completely in the wild. In other words, these programs—which may be run by universities, risk capital providers, sometimes successful entrepreneurs, or even large organizations such as your own—are making innovation more systematic, albeit within an ecosystem context. These more organized programs also add a sense of time pressure to the innovation cycles and ensure that resources are more effectively deployed. With this programmatic support, ecosystems become even more densely populated as they attract people who have novel ideas and ambitions for large-scale impact.

Perhaps the most iconic such program is Y Combinator (YC). It was founded in 2005 as the first so-called *start-up accelerator*, drawing from the experience of university start-up summer programs and VC practices, brought together to more systematically support the early-stage growth of new ventures. Starting in Boston but now closely associated with Silicon Valley, this for-profit accelerator focused on supporting what it labeled a *cohort* of early-stage founders through a single intensive, three-month experimentation cycle. As of this writing, YC has supported over four thousand start-ups, with close to a one hundred of them becoming *unicorns* with well-known names such as Stripe (the financial transactions company), AirBnB (changing the nature of hotel accommodation), and Dropbox (for cloud-based file sharing, such as drafts of this book) founded by MIT alum Drew Houston.

The cohort approach, based in a single location, provides a dense community of entrepreneurs (who gather at regular retreats and meetups) experimenting with novel ideas with some key resources. On the financial side, each start-up gets $500,000 (at the time of writing) from YC in return for an equity stake in the form of a SAFE. Other YC resources include mentors (available in group and one-on-one office hours) who support founders with the significant pressure to experiment and learn. At the end of the accelerator experience, a final *demo day*—a widely anticipated and competitive event—results in some of the most promising ventures being selected for further funding by VCs who have been mentors or who are in the audience.

On YC's seventh birthday, founder Paul Graham described his initial thinking:

> I had been telling [my colleague] . . . all the things they should change about the VC business—essentially the ideas now underlying Y Combinator [YC]: investors should be making more, smaller investments, they should be funding hackers instead of suits, they should be willing to fund younger founders, etc. Initially we only had part of the idea. We were going to do seed funding with standardized terms. Before YC, seed funding was very haphazard.
>
> Initially we didn't have what turned out to be the most important idea: funding start-ups synchronously, instead of asynchronously as it had always been done before. We got lucky in that the length and structure of a summer program turns out to be perfect for what we do: a summer program for undergrads seemed the fastest way to do it. No one takes summer jobs that seriously. The opportunity cost for a bunch of undergrads to spend a summer working on start-ups was low enough that we wouldn't feel guilty encouraging them to do it. . . . The structure of the YC cycle is still almost identical to what it was that first summer.[5]

The past twenty years have produced a dizzying array of other programs that in one way or another provide start-up teams—within universities and elsewhere—in the early stages of their inception-to-impact journey with a community, specialized resources, the opportunities to experiment, and the time-bounded pressures to manage experiments effectively. The programs, depending on their emphasis, support and develop early-stage *proto-ventures* (i.e., those that are founded and others not even fully or formally founded) in exploring and validating their novel products and services through fully formed, incorporated start-up ventures accelerating their experiments to scaling their ideas.

While traditionally optimized for the rapid cycles of digital ventures, programs that support innovation have also emerged to support deep-tech ventures, with their longer, more costly cycles. Examples include the US National Science Foundation's I-Corps, the Activate programs founded at the Lawrence Berkeley Lab, and The Engine built by MIT, whose Whiteboard and Blueprint programs help deep-tech founders turn their science-based ideas into start-up ventures, and then support their exploring and validating (respectively) ahead of potential investment.[6]

Even some more traditional venture funds have shifted toward more structured, systematic venture building. Most notable is Flagship Pioneering, whose founder Dr. Noubar Afeyan has transformed *venture building* in the life sciences by developing in-house *proto-ventures* (i.e., venture ideas that are too early and nascent to be incorporated as formal ventures but worth exploring as a potential proto-venture). The most notable venture to come through Flagship's *venture studio* process is Moderna, the start-up venture whose innovation in mRNA design and delivery led to one of the earliest and most successful COVID-19 vaccines.[7]

Innovation programs do some of the heavy lifting around the identification of novelty, accumulation of some specialized resources that start-ups need, and even the shaping of experimentation cycles into manageable, synchronized cycles. They structure what the participants will do and how they will interact, as well as define expectations for milestones. By configuring resources to support but also intensify innovation cycles through structured activities and reduced frictions to accessing resources and advice, these ecosystem programs aim to speed up the early cycles of innovation. They also help founders and their teams determine whether they have a good idea or not, by bringing more rigorous and systematic selection criteria to people and ideas—an approach that can feel quite competitive but means that teams have more rapid feedback and evaluation than they might otherwise have working alone in the classic entrepreneurial garage. As such, these developments in external innovation ecosystems have evolved several practices useful for those trying to achieve innovation internally.

Unfortunately, some of these programs have also had downsides, which are a matter of concern. Chief among these have been the biases that are as striking in these programs as they are in the wild of the ecosystem (and wider economy). Narrowing the diversity of those involved in innovation limits the sorts of people who flourish in innovation ecosystems. Most importantly, by focusing resources on entrepreneurs who only "look the part," innovation ecosystems risk reducing the novelty that they are aiming to encourage (if we assume that different sorts of ideas are often associated with different sorts of people). Leaders of ecosystem programs, along with those of you in large organizations, must be aware of the role of bias if you wish to optimize the return on innovation efforts, either internally or externally. The value of more systematic innovation programs provides a context in which to design bias out in a more intentional fashion. (See the sidebar for the research related to these biases.)

Bias in Innovation and Entrepreneurship

While bias occurs in many facets of human endeavor, its negative impact on innovation, and the results you may be seeking, make it worth addressing here. Let's look at the research behind just one example of bias, namely gender discrimination, to surface the issue that can itself be a first step toward improving the situation. Our studies demonstrate that selection processes can systematically treat start-ups with male or female leaders differently, with negative consequences for female-led ones.

In an experiment that provided decision makers with identical start-up pitches, that differed only with the gender of the voice-over on the pitch deck slides, the audience was almost twice as likely to find the male entrepreneur convincing and investible.[8] In another study by colleagues at Columbia University, female entrepreneurs were more likely to be asked questions about what might go wrong with their idea, while male entrepreneurs were asked what could go right.

In yet other analysis, working with our friend and colleague Dr. Mercedes Delgado, we find that, while women have made great inroads into science and engineering PhD programs, they still are not included at parity in university patenting (either while as students or later as faculty).[9]

In some ways, these outcomes (especially for venture funding) are the result of those making selection choices facing the high level of uncertainty already involved with early-stage ventures by choosing entrepreneurs or innovators who look or sound the part, or who are similar to successful entrepreneurs who have come before. These heuristic "rules of thumb" or unconscious choices will, however, result in suboptimal outcomes: the lower participation of diverse innovators and entrepreneurs means less novelty for our ecosystems and for our organizations, and thus fewer new solutions for the essential challenges and priorities we confront. If leaders are seeking to optimize their return on innovation, and find the best problem/solution matches, then systematically undervaluing those from half the population is likely to be suboptimal.

Newly designed programs are emerging—including some to deal explicitly with these and other barriers to participation. As leaders in large organizations, you should be conscious of the effect that biases and barriers can have, and assess your potential programs with this in mind.

Well-designed ecosystem programs are increasingly aware of biases, so more aim to explicitly attract and crowd in large numbers and more diverse potential participants and then have a wide range of approaches to selecting them. As a result, they have become the most effective way for leaders in large organizations to identify the right entrepreneurs and innovators in an otherwise messy and scattered environment. It therefore makes sense for you to work with these programs, at least initially, when you are new to innovation or to a specific ecosystem, as they are "watering holes" where like-minded entrepreneurs gather. With increasing experience, commitment, and risk tolerance, you may partner with the programs more extensively, or then even try to run such programs yourselves, drawing on internal organizational talent as well as potentially drawing in people from the ecosystem (or perhaps a mix).

The rest of this section explains a broad categorization of the different types of programs and the benefits they are likely to yield, according to the innovation cycles that they support. This is important for ecosystem engagement, as "what" you want should inform the type of program (i.e., the "how") that you should engage.

Understanding the distinctions among them will help you determine which programs align with your "what"—your organization's priorities—and your "who"—your decisions about the people you should engage. If you

	Exploring	**Validating**	**Accelerating**	**Scaling**
Programs	Hackathons & Bootcamps	Competitions & Venture Studios	Accelerators	Venture Funds
Program (& Other) Funding	Small prizes, Small awards, some friends, & family money	Grants and awards (can range up to large $$$), small equity investments	SAFEs or early equity, as well as prizes (for success in accelerator) or grants	Equity Series A, B, etc. from investors & some Work Programs (from government)

Figure 4.4
Mapping ecosystem programs and funding to the innovation "cycles."

participate in a program focused on exploring but are hoping for ideas to channel into the growth stages of your innovation pipeline for revenue growth, you'll be disappointed. Similarly, if you work with a program focused on digital-tech ventures when you are really seeking deep-tech solutions, you may find it a poor use of time. As we illustrate in figure 4.4, particular programs are generally found at specific cycles and typically seek to support those cycles in innovation ecosystems.

In our framework, we start with programs that support the very earliest cycles of idea generation (i.e., exploring)—these include hackathons and bootcamps (exemplified by Start-up Weekend, which Techstars founded in Boulder, Colorado in 2007).[10] We then move to programs that support longer cycles of validating, that is problem/solution matching. Those with an emphasis on solution generation include competitions, challenges that can result in grants, or prizes such as the X Prize. Also, in this early stage are other competitive programs that instead emphasize problem generation and de-risking against a solution, including so-called venture studios like the UK's Founders Factory.

Our third cycle emphasizes accelerating and thus includes accelerator programs that support venture building, including YC, MC in Greater Boston, and many corporate accelerators such as Aramco's LAB7, Barclays'

Rise, and Philips Health. The final group of programs, focused on scaling ventures, includes various outfits that offer more open-ended support that helps start-ups scale their products and their businesses but with a focus on different sorts of VC, especially corporate VC.

Let us consider each of these four cycles, with the various program options.

Cycle 1: Exploring Phase, through Hackathons and Bootcamps

The early innovation cycle of *exploring* is increasingly supported by programs often known as hackathons and bootcamps, which are intensive opportunities to generate ideas (that is *ideating*) and be creative. They range from hackathons that last just twenty-four hours, which people sometimes liken to a sprint, to bootcamps that last the better part of a week but have a similar goal in mind, and variations in between. (At MIT, we run a week-long hackathon for executives, who commit twenty-four hours spread across several workday afternoons, after morning lectures, to explore their start-up ideas.)

At a hackathon, participants will "hack" away at a problem: suggesting an idea, winning others to their team, iterating rapidly through several hypothetical problem/solution matches, and pitching solutions. These are often run for students. In the most traditional hackathons, which focus on software, students code solutions. Others like "Hacking Disabilities" at MIT ask participants to work on making better designs for everyday devices and tools. Inside a large organization, you might focus participants on specific internal challenges, like improving back-office processes, reducing bureaucracy, or exploring new ways to engage customers.

At bootcamps, participants might bring their own ideas or focus on a particular problem domain. The main difference from a hackathon is that, over the course of a week, participants can learn more entrepreneurial tools: how to do *primary market research* (PMR) and then *primary customer research* (PCR), and how to define *user journeys*, use *design thinking* methods, or even design *minimum viable products* (MVPs). At the end of either program, participants demonstrate their solutions (on a workshop's last day, it's a *demo day*), with a short (usually five-minute) pitch from which judges choose winners.

Hackathons can cover a range of topics. For example, leaders from Lockheed Martin cohosted a "Tech for Truth" hackathon at MIT in 2019. With three tracks focused on tech for humanitarian aid, combating fake news, and supply chain integrity, the hackathon program attracted over 250 students and other community participants to work with Lockheed's corporate executives over a weekend. The winners got to attend the prestigious SXSW (South by Southwest) conference in Austin, Texas. Meanwhile, Lockheed's leadership team got exposure to new talent, fresh perspectives, and novel ways to approach their existing challenges, giving them a return on their investment.

A short hackathon or a longer bootcamp, whether run internally or externally, will bring you tremendous energy, inspiration, and wealth of talent to the challenges of interest to you. For example, Lockheed was intrigued by the number of young people who were inspired by the mission of using technology for good, especially to combat misinformation, and realized that they might change their hiring approaches to use hackathons more systematically as a recruiting and talent-spotting tool. However, it won't produce a completed product and new revenue stream.

Similarly, a bootcamp run internally by large organizations or with a mix of internal and external talent can give you an opportunity to see your younger employees in action alongside more established organizational leaders. The tangible output from both types of *exploring* programs is often a power point presentation that the team might wish to take into the next innovation cycle if there is sufficient interest on the part of their sponsor or the team themselves. On the other hand, the hackathon may create less tangible outputs, such as building new connections among people who had not met before and really establishing links from your organization into a community of innovators. Participants, after doing well at a hackathon or bootcamp, might go on to develop their ideas inside your organization or in an ecosystem, and later in their life cycle may win a place in a formal accelerator program (see the accelerating cycle).

Cycle 2: Validating Phase, through Prizes and Challenges

Validating new, more well-formulated opportunities can often happen effectively through programs such as prizes or challenges that are associated with a cycle beyond hackathons. Because they tend to focus on generating solutions to well-specified problems, they can be a powerful means to explore a clear gap in a large organization's innovation portfolio.

Typically, these competition programs often last three to six months, especially if internal (or it can sometimes be a little more open-ended, especially if external, awaiting a winning solution). The elements of such challenges have remained remarkably similar over the centuries. One of the most famous and successful historical examples of a "prize competition" is the Longitude Prize of 1714, which we referenced at the beginning of this chapter and still holds lessons for today. The problem the British government faced in the early eighteenth century was that their navigators could not determine their longitudinal position in the world.[11] Most experts of the day, the (literal) "big wigs," assumed that the solution lay in better astronomy. Most efforts to that point had focused on attempting to determine longitude by the stars, though these solutions had all failed.

Instead, the people who designed the 1714 competition—including Sir Isaac Newton—wisely decided to take a different path and avoided specifying a solution. And the winner of the Longitude Prize was not an astronomer but a clockmaker from north England, who created a remarkably accurate timepiece (made of wood, so as to survive being at sea). The core principles of the contest—define the problem, be open to creative solutions, and reward unconventional expertise—have survived the test of time and really do emphasize the early validating cycle of innovation.

Challenge programs such as prizes and competitions work best, in fact, when they elicit ideas from a wide range of talented people who are driven by enthusiasm and a desire to compete. Our work has shown that prizes, ranging from the Ansari X Prize (awarded for the first nongovernment organization to launch a reusable crewed spacecraft into space twice within two weeks) to the Hyperloop Pod Competition launched by Elon Musk's SpaceX, attract a wide range of talented people who are driven by enthusiasm, competitiveness, and a desire to win. In the case of Hyperloop, a tremendous wealth of talent emerged over the five years of the competition—especially, and unexpectedly, from the German ecosystem around TUM in Munich. SpaceX then hired many of these individuals to support its own internal innovation or, occasionally, ideas that it might have sought to license.[12]

As with most innovation programs, there are two main choices: run your own or leverage someone else's. Here, the case of Hyperloop is instructive: obviously, the main benefits accrued to SpaceX. That said, the sponsors of the teams from the TUM, ETH Zurich (which also spun out Auterion), and others also learned from their engagement with the teams as they sought out extraordinary talent and other resources. For those in large organizations seeking innovation from the ecosystem, such challenges can also be launched directly. For some government agencies such as the UK's Ministry of Defence, using competitions (led by DASA, its Defence and Security Accelerator) is an opportunity to tap into talented teams and reasonably well-developed ideas. They then need to find ways to work together after the competition is over to accelerate and scale solutions to some of the defense community's most pressing problems.

For example, DASA's Intelligent Ship competition hoped to find submissions to design, optimize, and demonstrate Human-Autonomy Team collaborations in a marine context, seeking to find and shape solutions from the UK ecosystem.[13] Not new to competitions and challenges, the US's DARPA started using competitions in the early 2000s with its Grand Challenge for autonomous vehicles. Corporates can do the same, and like governments, they must factor in the costs, that is, not just the prize but also the staff costs of running the challenges and the cost of testing the solutions that are presented.

By sharing problems, the large organizations often ran the risk of alerting competitors of their business strategy. That said, whatever your large organization's problems and challenges, competitions are an exciting way to find people with novel ideas who are not necessarily the usual suspects you'd typically talk to. And conversely, these talented people may not be aware that you have so many intriguing priorities and opportunities to explore together.

While prizes and challenges focus on validating solutions to very well-specified problems, another type of competition-focused program is the early *venture studio* (sometimes known as a *venture builder*). This program explores and then defines solutions in a problem space, wider market, or particular context more widely, in the hope of developing several competing hypotheses that might become ventures. Many different ventures are proposed within the studio and are sometimes referred to as *proto-ventures* until a smaller number are selected to be accelerated and scaled as formal ventures.

Sometimes these efforts focus on opportunities in a particular context such as healthcare. This approach has been refined and scaled by Flagship Pioneering, using its own internal postdoctoral fellows and executives in residence to define solutions to novel health challenges and develop a series of proto-ventures to be potentially released into the ecosystem. Entrepreneurs have used this type of program to build a community and ecosystem in places with few start-ups, such as Rocket Internet in Berlin. Entrepreneur

First, started in London, has expanded to Paris, Bangalore, and New York, and it emphasizes finding young talented individuals and giving them a structured opportunity to build teams and ideas and ultimately define and start to build ventures in areas they are committed to. Amir Basoum, who is now based between the US and Egypt, has also founded a venture studio to focus on AI in healthcare. Like other successful entrepreneurs, he sees the studio as a way to extend his impact by validating a range of different exciting ventures, not just one.

Some large organizations have copied this approach. For example, the DARPA entrepreneur-in-residence program helps bring founders into labs to define ventures from DARPA-funded solutions. A fascinating example, well documented in his online book, is the journey by Standard Chartered (SC) bank's Alex Manson, who created SC Ventures—the bank's approach to creating a series of programmatic activities to build ventures that redefine the industry. Describing his 2018 meeting with the bank's CEO, Alex noted the following:

> Bill and I invented a new unit of the Bank, to be called "SC Ventures." It would include the eXellerator lab, which had been spearheading innovation in the Bank with fintech engagement. It would also involve a Human-Centred Design (HCD) curriculum, and SC Studios—a small scouting office in San Francisco. We wanted to design a way to invest in fintech. . . . The eXellerator, the Innovation Investment Fund and the Ventures became the "three pillars" of SC Ventures, which we launched in March 2018. . . . In designing SC Ventures and its three pillars, we were betting that, while any one of the efforts would be insufficient to have a transformational impact by itself, the combination of the three actually would.[14]

The SC approach provides internal support—in the form of a studio, if you will—for *intrapreneurs* (internal entrepreneurs) to define business ventures that have the potential to transform their business. Programs like this also strongly rely on gaining internal support from within business units and then making choices about whether the ventures will remain internal or be spun out. In the case of SC, if successful, they can graduate into their internal accelerator. However, for corporations, such (early) venture studios provide an opportunity to define and develop new in-house ventures—either around internal solutions (IP or other ideas) or perhaps drawing widely to define solutions to clearly identified problems. It is an opportunity to give internal employees, or entrepreneurs coming in from the outside, a chance to work in a time-bounded fashion on developing the venture.

Cycle 3: Accelerating Phase, for Example Accelerators Driving toward Impact

Accelerator programs typically support projects that have completed the first two cycles. By cycle 3, entrepreneurs will have explored problem and solution spaces. They have a defined proposal, often with a prototype, perhaps even something they can share with customers that suggests they have validated the basic elements of their idea. Now they need the resources to accelerate the innovation process and turn it into a proof of concept or actual product.

Accelerators take what can be a rather lonely process of building a business in the wild of the ecosystem and instead assemble a cohort of entrepreneurs who will both collaborate and compete for three or more months in the hopes that this intensive experience will indeed accelerate their journey. Although accelerators can target any stage in the innovation cycle, they typically support projects that are at, or just past, the *proof-of-concept* stage and so focus on providing office or lab space, as well as more specialized resources and mentoring. The details of these accelerator programs vary according to the sector and type of technology, but the emphasis is on the resources, the cohort (which allows for learning across teams), and, again, the time pressure. Some, like YC and MC (which we met earlier), are quite general in the IDEs that they admit to their core program. Others are more focused, like Starburst in Paris and Los Angeles for aerospace ventures and Seraphim in London, for entrepreneurs interested in the challenges of space (from satellite-based earth observation to in-space manufacturing and weather).

Accelerators provide funding, either in the form of small equity investments (on which they expect a return, such as YC), grants and prizes (which is MC's approach and the approach followed by DeltaV, which is one of MIT's on-campus accelerators for students), or, less often, as sponsorship. They gather in resources from the ecosystem—such as start-up advice from successful entrepreneurs, mentoring from corporate members, and resources from risk capital providers—so that the venture-building teams can focus on accelerating progress through their experimental cycle. In contrast to the earlier-cycle programs, accelerators are intended to push the venture to an outcome: a growth target, a decision about a key market segment, or to stop working on an idea.[15]

Large organizations wanting to engage with serious start-up ventures on the cusp of accelerating toward key milestones benefit from the accelerators' efficiency at attracting a large number of start-up ventures focused on a problem or solution domain. This allows them to pick a start-up that interests them, with a sufficient level of commitment, resources, and novelty to be relevant to their internal priorities. If you follow the path of a company like Philips Healthcare in Boston, you will see it engage with an external accelerator, alongside MassMutual and Massachusetts General Hospital (MGH). This provides it with a focused program in partnership with Mass-Challenge aimed at accelerating high impact start-ups in digital health, where they can swiftly see a lot of ideas, and find those that are relevant to strategic priorities.

Accelerator programs are increasingly widespread among large corporates themselves with these organizations (such as the previously mentioned Standard Chartered) building their own accelerator and others, like Mercedes-Benz or some of the larger oil majors, partnering with a range of other large organizations to build an industry-wide platform.

Working to build their own accelerator, global mining conglomerate BHP established its Xplor Accelerator to find entrepreneurial talent and novel solutions for early-stage critical mineral exploration ventures. The organization, which has mines in Western Australia, Canada, Chile, and beyond (including in iron ore, copper, and nickel), has provided funding (up to $500,000), technical and commercial coaching, and a chance to pitch for follow-on funding or partnerships with BHP.[16]

Taking a more industry-wide approach, Mercedes-Benz—the automotive maker in Stuttgart, Germany—worked in 2016 with Plug and Play and the University of Stuttgart to establish the Startup Autobahn accelerator. Over time, other corporate partners have joined the accelerator as Mercedes-Benz recognized that deep collaboration in building it with Porsche and Bridgestone, along with Bosch and BASF, brought additional benefits. The accelerator focuses on start-ups with software solutions for mobility but includes opportunities to explore deep-tech themes, such as innovations in battery development, new materials, and biometrics. Startup Autobahn is structured around a cadence that includes a scouting phase, a selection day, a one-hundred-day pilot phase, and finally a closing expo demo day—once again mimicking the sorts of rapid innovation cycles that we find to be an essential feature of innovation ecosystems.

For corporate partners, participation in initial selection, and then mentoring, judging, and networking with the start-up founders, is an important opportunity to streamline and structure ecosystem engagement. As Startup Autobahn itself says, partner benefits include scouting for new ideas that match your organizational challenge, building a network of like-minded partners (with other large corporates and start-up entrepreneurs), and, importantly, shaping their internal innovation culture by working closely with start-ups in new ways.[17]

Governments have also engaged, partnered with, and led accelerators. The Dubai Future Foundation is a leading example, with its program running accelerators focused on challenges in government services, including "The Future of AI in Government Services."[18] Start-ups are attracted to its equity-free business model, as the participating public agencies have chosen not to take a stake in the start-up ventures. For the Dubai government, it has been an opportunity to connect to start-ups in areas ranging from traffic analytics to smart monitoring for services that include transportation, wastewater treatment, and energy usage. Most recently, the Dubai Center for AI has partnered with the Dubai Futures Foundation to work with thirty start-up ventures on developing AI solutions to government ministry challenges around efficiency and productivity.

Cycle 4: Scaling Phase (to Grow Ventures to Scale)

The final phase is *scaling* the venture. In the wilds of the external ecosystem, this is achieved in various ways. Most approaches are not as time bounded as earlier cycles, primarily because each venture will have unique time and capital needs as it builds out its novel solutions across regions, countries, and continents (recall that deep tech takes much longer to develop than digital tech, which can scale rapidly after the accelerating phase). That said, VC funds often support start-ups in this cycle, typically providing equity financing from Series A onward for experiments that end (if successful) with the venture commercializing its products at scale and ultimately being acquired or going public.

Engaging innovators at this stage of innovation requires working directly with start-up ventures or with their VC investors. As noted in the previous chapter, if your organization is an LP in a venture fund or a potential investor, you can engage with the frontline partners and GPs in these funds and understand whether their investments are in the areas that matter to your company. (And you can visit the VCs' quiet, luxurious, and sometimes quirky office spaces, occasionally complete with scented candles!)

Although the scaling phase of venture funding and engagement is not always time bounded across a cohort of ventures or projects (as programs are in the earlier cycles), VC funding is, as we have said, a staged and milestone-based activity. As such, we wanted to include these programs in our analysis. Large organizations in both the public and private sectors increasingly use VC techniques themselves, directly making equity investments through their own corporate venture capital (CVC) units or (for governments) via their country's *strategic investment fund* (SIF), which can be funded in various ways including from a *sovereign wealth fund* (SWF). If you are seeking to use VC techniques to pursue your organization's strategic priorities (rather than simply to provide financial returns), then these strategic funds should not, however, try to only mimic traditional freestanding VC firms that just seek financial outcomes.

Our experience shows that you and your CVC/SIF team will be more successful in making a relevant contribution to your organization's (or department's) innovation efforts if you are focused on executing investments that are built to be a distinct but important part of your organization's innovation portfolio and clearly aligned with the strategic goals of the investors (whether they are represented by your board, your senior leaders, or your treasury or a government department). These sorts of strategically aligned funds, in contrast to a more isolated return-making vehicle, tend to survive longer within large complex organizations.

Leaders should therefore not expect their strategic investments in innovation to necessarily achieve the same level of profit-maximizing returns as standard financially focused VC firms. For strategic risk capital, the benefit of a CVC or SIF is not simply about a reasonable rate of return on that capital (perhaps facilitating a later acquisition of the venture by the large organization's M&A unit). Instead, companies or government agencies with a venture fund can use it to make targeted, well-structured investments in start-ups with a focus that aligns with the organization in one of three different ways:

- Start-ups in the PN zone that are adapting solutions that can help you solve novel problems. An example is BHP's venture arm leading the investment in Plotlogic, using AI scanning technology to extract critical minerals from old mines—a new problem and adaptation of existing machine learning and imaging technologies to this valuable geological challenge. From the government side, BDC Capital (the venture-funding arm of the Development Bank of Canada) has recently invested in the digital analytical company Arolytics, adapting digital solutions to the challenges of the oil and gas industry's methane management.

- Start-ups in the SN zone that are developing extremely novel solutions to problems that you are familiar with but with emerging technology that is outside the scope of your own internal R&D efforts. One example is Eni's VC investment in Bob Mumgaard's CFS. Likewise, the UK's National Security SIF (NSSIF) invested in Oxford Ionics—a quantum computing company—to ensure that the company could benefit from patient capital (more willing to support longer innovation cycles) as it develops solutions to important dual-use problems.

- Start-ups in the N^2 zone that are building novel solutions to exciting, new problems where you want to have a seat at the table to learn and shape the direction of the venture as the space-based economy expands. A good example is Boeing's investment in Natalya Bailey's Accion Systems. Turning to the government side, the Saudi-based NEOM Investment Fund—a fund supporting the growth of economic sectors in the new NEOM region—has invested in ZeroAvia, a start-up venture building new prototype planes with novel hydrogen electric engines that are reducing aviation's climate impact.

Leaders should measure these strategic funds based on returning strategic benefits to the organization (or government). In doing so, they are more likely to find common cause with the entrepreneurial founders because they can work in close partnership, providing resources and opportunities for experimentation that the wider ecosystem might not find as easy to galvanize, especially in the later, more specialized cycles.

Using VC-like programs to support your organization's engagement with the innovation ecosystem at the later innovation cycles is not unique to large private sector corporations, as we have noted in our examples above. The UK's NSSIF invests in national-security-related ventures and technologies identified as critical strategic priorities by the government. By acting as a government CVC, the deal flow that the NSSIF leaders see through their continuous engagement with the ecosystem provides valuable insights into future technologies that can be fed back into departmental decision-making, thus bringing significant value into internal innovation portfolio decisions. Similarly, CVCs within the pharmaceutical industry help augment insights into the internal portfolio of new medicines across a wide range of therapeutic areas. Our colleague Pieter Wolters at DSM Venturing, whom we met at the start of this book, focuses on expanding insights and impact into health and nutrition in human and animal care.

Investments across the three zones all provide different sorts of opportunities to meet priorities, much as for the private sector. In the PN zone, VC-like investments can accompany specific contracts (sometimes called work programs) that are designed to fund adaptations of existing emerging technology solutions to a new government or a new corporate problem. In the SN zone, government VC investments can be useful to *crowd in* equity capital from the private sector in areas of strategic interest but where the time horizons to reach high-TRL solutions are long (e.g., in areas like quantum computing, encryption, and fusion). Third, especially in the N^2 zone, equity investments provide an ongoing window into novel problems, solutions, and matches that are likely to be of long-run strategic importance. Here, equity might be as much about getting a seat at the table, from which to view risks and opportunities and the emergence of a new industry, as it is about specific, narrowly defined outcomes: NEOM Investment Fund demonstrates this through its co-investment with Airbus, Barclays, AP Ventures, and BEV, among others.

Docking Ecosystem Innovation into Your Organization

Now that you have investigated the programs in your chosen ecosystem, you're ready to look back at your organization and identify how you might *pull through* this wealth of programmatic activity into its innovation pipeline. Recall from the beginning of this chapter that innovation cycles in the ecosystem are analogous to the stages in your internal pipeline—both punctuated by milestones (and opportunities to stop!). Ventures and projects move from one phase to the next, based on their results, with clear gates or selection filters. The process supports a wide set of ideas at the start, funneling them through the pipeline and then downselecting them.

Knowing how your external ecosystem activities should interact and dock with your internal innovation system pipeline is essential to effective ecosystem engagement. Most organizations that we have worked with struggle to ensure that their ecosystem engagements at various cycles are effectively linked into their internal innovation system.

To overcome this, we recommend an approach that looks at the docking process from two perspectives. First, it starts with aligning the stages of your internal pipeline with best practices from the cycles of the external ecosystem. Second, it requires linking external projects with the internal pipeline at the right stage, to facilitate *pull-through*. We have found that many leaders, once they understand the external ecosystem and its cycles, will restructure and align their internal innovation systems, and can only then work effectively through how to link external ideas into their newly designed internal system. In fact, this is the approach we recommend, as your external ideas will otherwise run into the buzzsaw of a poorly designed internal innovation system.

A detailed analysis of your internal pipeline and processes—their strengths and weaknesses, frictions and limitations, and the nature of your selection filters at various stage gates—is beyond this book's scope. However, your large organization can adapt key tools from the world of the innovation ecosystem, which are likely to be very compatible with your strategic priorities for innovation. Success hinges on recognizing the differences in the types of tools and experiments relevant in different zones of the problem/solution matrix and at different stages of innovation, thereby avoiding mere additions to innovation theater. Doing so can increase internal novelty and can help you match the resources that you do have to the right projects (even if these resources are not as widely varied and specialized as those in the external innovation ecosystem). It can also support a more structured, learning-focused approach to your stage-gate activities and help run more focused experiments, thus building a culture of experimentation.

In general, we recommend that you structure internal activities according to the *innovation cycle/stage* framework as a rough-and-ready way to align internal efforts with external practices. You would, for example, use internal hackathons for the *ideation* stage—something Boston-based Vertex, a pharmaceutical company, does each year. You could follow this with internal prize/challenge competitions or a venture studio for the validating (and validation) stage, as Google has done with its X program. For the next (i.e., accelerating) cycle, some organizations build internal accelerators (though they may take on other names), as Microsoft has with its M12 program.[19] Finally, there is the "scaling" (or growth) phase, where the venture or project will need financing for growth, whether through VC growth capital or internal investment.

CYCLES

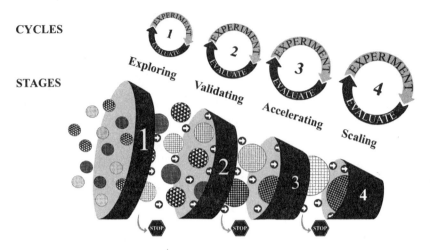

STAGES

Figure 4.5
Mapping the ecosystem's four cycles to the pipeline's four stages.

Once you have made some important adaptations to your internal innovation system, inspired by lessons from the external ecosystem, you are now in a position to consider how to dock your external engagement activities with the internal pipeline (see figure 4.5).

You can view the four phases of your external cycles in parallel with your four internal stages to see how your activities in each place line up. Be sure to include in your view the processes but also the people in the organization who connect with the ecosystem community through their participation in the various programs across the innovation cycle—such as the technology scouts and project leaders. (More on these humans later!)

To design the external/internal (outside/in) docking, you need to determine how the insights, ideas, people, and especially ventures from the ecosystem that address your strategic priorities (the "what") will be integrated into your organization's portfolio and at what stage. This is how you will access the value from the ecosystem, but doing so can be challenging. You need to make space in your internal innovation system to allow for integration at the appropriate point, often at a *stage gate* or milestone. There also need to be clear opportunities to insert ideas, *proto-ventures*, or entire ventures from the ecosystem into your innovation pipeline. Of course, docking might not mean completely merging them into your pipeline; indeed, you likely want to maintain some benefits of the external innovation ecosystem.

However, you will probably still wish to deepen the integration into your internal activities, whether through providing more resources (e.g., people or funding), by establishing a contract for a pilot demonstration in one of your facilities or with your customers, or ultimately by pursuing a more formal joint venture or acquisition later.

The key to a successful internal innovation system is to identify decision points, use consistent language, and create a portfolio of internal and external choices that align with your priorities—the **what** that you painstakingly laid out in chapter 2. The reverse is also true when you reach a stage gate in your internal pipeline: you have an opportunity to move your work to the ecosystem through a *spinout* (more likely in the case of a government lab or corporate R&D center) or at a later cycle with a new line of business that has potential but does not fit your strategic road map.

For example, at the end of the *exploring* cycle, whether from the first external cycle (in the ecosystem) or the first internal stage (of your pipeline), you will decide whether to move to the validating and validation phase. In the ecosystem, you might see the result of an external hackathon or bootcamp and decide to hire the person or team involved to conduct the next phase of idea development in-house. Or you might encourage them on their journey into an accelerator and just remain in contact. Internally, your team may conclude that it lacks expertise to move further and decide to seek novelty from an ecosystem.

Following the *validating* cycle, you might have a prototype. If developed internally, you may not have the specialized infrastructure needed for accelerating the project. It might be worthwhile for the team to bring the idea to an accelerator in the ecosystem, perhaps as part of your venture studio activities. Alternatively, if you find a venture in the ecosystem with a promising prototype, you could support that team as it demonstrates its potential with a more refined prototype and experiments with your customers or one of your operational sites.

At the accelerating and scaling cycles, your CVC/SIF can make a direct investment in a novel venture from the ecosystem that delivers value to your organization. This decision might be accompanied by a partnership agreement to work on a specific program with a business unit or with a mission-delivery team that might also be a first customer of the venture through a *work program*. Conversely, you might spin out an idea (perhaps with a seat on the board or taking equity) if you want to maintain links and interactions with a previously internal team but do not believe the project is a good fit for your current internal portfolio. (Such a spinout opportunity could help retain your entrepreneurial staff who might progress their ideas outside, perhaps on a secondment. Whether the venture works out or not, these employees could have the right to return, like academic faculty on a sabbatical.)

These considerations about docking will be especially important for projects in the three furthest horizon zones. If you have a range of projects across the entire portfolio and you run the pipeline differently for different types of projects by zone, you are likely to accommodate more ideas more effectively than if you force every project to follow the same process. Projects with high problem-novelty and low solution-novelty (in the PN zone) will have different cycles, timelines, and experiments than those with low problem-novelty and high solution-novelty (in the SN zone), and even more than the high-risk, exciting N^2 zone projects.

Of course, regardless of the design of your internal pipeline and the way you dock external ecosystem activities into your internal milestones and priorities, you need people in the right places with the authority to make decisions about the innovations your organization will pursue, with whom, and how. The next chapter shows you the types of leaders you need, and their roles, to ensure that your organization can benefit from the external ecosystem. You will need focused leadership at the top, middle, and bottom to successfully integrate external innovation and add value to BAU.

Key Points from Chapter 4: How to Engage in an Ecosystem

Having determined "who" your large organization needs to engage, it is important to clarify "how" to do so given the dynamic nature of multi-stakeholder ecosystems, where various elements and interactions are key:

- Innovation *cycles* represent the underlying processes in the wild of ecosystems, for each of which there are relevant purposes, practices, and programs.
- Each cycle is effectively an experiment, which is evaluated and results in downselection, with a few ventures going into the next cycle but with more resources.
- In a four-cycle model, it is possible to match them to common ecosystem programs:

- ○ 1 is **exploring**, as found in *hackathons* (where *ideas* are quickly explored)
- ○ 2 is **validating**, as found in prizes, challenges, and venture studios
- ○ 3 is **accelerating**, as found in accelerator programs (not pure incubators)
- ○ 4 is **scaling**, as found in CVC or sovereign investment funds (for companies and governments, respectively)
- In the ecosystem, stakeholders play a role in the competitive, Darwinian process of downselection, so only ideas with the best fit are likely to survive.
- Large organizations often replicate these phases with similar internal practices:
  - ○ usually known as *stages* along a *pipeline* (with *stage gates* in between) but usually without the ecosystem's competitive downselection process and sometimes without clarity about value created by each milestone
- One challenge with *pull-through* of innovation from ecosystem engagement is knowing how the external cycles might best "dock" with those of the internal stages.

Turning to chapter 5, we now discuss the role of leadership in ecosystem engagement.

5 Leadership for Ecosystem Engagement

Effective ecosystem engagement requires thoughtful leadership from top to bottom. Without it, your efforts will be wasted. Worse, you may alienate potential partners, and your reputation as a forward-looking organization in the ecosystem may suffer. In other words, the stakes can be high. But getting it right challenges many organizations and frustrates even the most focused of leaders.

Belinda, the government agency leader you met earlier, was responsible for choosing an employee to identify entrepreneurs who might be interested in solving some of her team's sensitive mission-critical problems. What was the profile she needed? We suggested that the right employee would have an appreciation of, and enthusiasm for, start-up ventures and be willing to describe these internal challenges to committed external entrepreneurs. The first person she put on the job built some strong relationships with entrepreneurs, but they did not have close ties with her internal teams. Their ability to translate what the entrepreneurs offered into the agency's needs was limited.

The next person—Abby—was more successful. She had a stellar reputation internally, with strong aspirations for a long-term career inside the organization, a fascination for hackathons, and a willingness to learn about the challenges of start-ups. Abby was also an excellent *tech scout*, able to blend into local venture meetups and bootcamps. But she was so busy focusing on the entrepreneurs that she did not have time to appreciate and engage with risk capital providers and accelerator leaders (who were likely to be some of Belinda's best conduits into the innovation ecosystem, as they saw so much deal flow). She needed another person to work with—someone who could talk knowledgeably about Belinda's organizational challenges as opportunities and could connect with VCs and later-stage entrepreneurs.

Like Belinda, you will need different people to engage with different stakeholders in the ecosystem. University relationship managers used to working with senior faculty members in an institutional setting are likely to find little in common with recently minted PhD entrepreneurs, and so they might need to be paired with young technical managers who have only recently left academia for that aspect of university engagement. Leading a corporate venture unit requires a deeper appreciation of the entrepreneurial journey, especially the early cycles from exploring to accelerating, in addition to investment acumen and an understanding of your strategic needs. You wouldn't choose the same person for this role as you would to run an M&A team that works to acquire later-stage businesses, and so on. None of these choices really matters if your ecosystem engagement is more about innovation theater. However, if you want to roll up your sleeves and use an ecosystem to add value to some of your most pressing priorities, then your choice of people and your wider organizational choices are essential to your success.

This chapter shows you how to set up your organization to support the "what, who, and how" of ecosystem engagement. We look in detail at the people involved: what leaders at different levels of the organization contribute, who they are and the characteristics they need to succeed, and the ways to help ensure success over the long term, after the initial flurry of engagement is completed.

Leadership from the Senior, Middle, and Frontline Levels

Leadership is not the sole preserve of senior executives: Belinda, Kristo (the defense ministry leader), John (the insurance executive), Pieter from DSM Venturing, and others we have met are essential, but they aren't enough.

Research from our colleague Professor Deborah Ancona has shown that *distributed leadership*—giving responsibility to individuals at multiple levels within the hierarchy—is more effective in times of turbulence and uncertainty than top-down command and control.[1] This is especially true if you are innovating at the far innovation horizon. There, people closest to the work (and closest to the ideas), who can rapidly understand and assess changes to the opportunities and risks of projects, are best positioned to make decisions about whether and how to proceed with them.

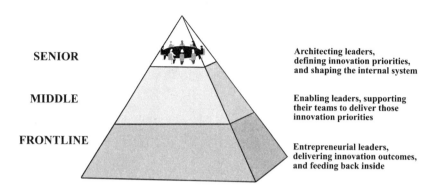

SENIOR

MIDDLE

FRONTLINE

Architecting leaders,
defining innovation priorities,
and shaping the internal system

Enabling leaders, supporting
their teams to deliver those
innovation priorities

Entrepreneurial leaders,
delivering innovation outcomes,
and feeding back inside

Figure 5.1
Levels of leadership to drive innovation in your organization.

More recently, Deborah has described a three-level leadership pyramid for nimble and innovation-oriented organizations.[2] Building on her work, we elaborate on these three levels of leadership for roles pursuing innovation inside your organization system (and for leading your ecosystem engagement), as follows, set out in figure 5.1.

- Senior-level leaders play an "architecting" role. These executives set the strategic direction for innovation and architect the design—including the processes and workflow—of the innovation organization. They set priorities, choose people to fill key roles, and empower them to manage the innovation process internally and externally. They will often have titles like chief innovation officer, head of R&D, chief strategy officer, or chief of external innovation.

- Middle-level leaders play an "enabling" role. These managers—ideally with experience of the organization's BAU and innovation work—interpret the directions of the senior leaders and report back to them. They also manage internal innovation processes, and shape and facilitate external engagement as they support and guide the leaders at the level below them. They have titles like managing director/head of ventures, head of innovation (working to a senior leader in the strategy function or for a particular region), or head of innovation lab(s).

- Frontline leaders play an "entrepreneurial" role. These employees execute elements of the ecosystem engagement strategy, with a focus on finding and shepherding ideas. They are usually experts in a problem or solution area. They may be in staff rather than management positions, but they are responsible for recommending actions to the middle-level managers above them. They might be called an ecosystem lead, head of external entrepreneurship (if it is an activity with few or no reports), or accelerator program manager.

Up to now, we have asked the "what, who, and how" questions about the ecosystem from the inside, looking out: what the organization needs, who can provide it (and where), and how to access the ideas that address its priorities. However, successful ecosystem engagement requires reciprocity. Leaders must look back at their organizations from the outside and ask "What do we bring to the ecosystem?," "Who are our best people to engage with external stakeholders?," and "How do we ensure that our external innovation efforts complement what we are doing internally?"

This outside-in perspective should bring sharp focus on whether you need to evolve how you do innovation internally and, importantly, whether you must put some new leaders in place to run your internal and external innovation activities. Doing so can disrupt the social networks of the organization and its culture. We will discuss how to address unease about, and possibly even opposition to, innovation within the wider organization in the next chapter. For now, let's look at the people you need in your innovation organization and how they should lead in ways that align with your internal priorities and with the external ecosystem.

Leading for the "What": Setting Innovation Priorities

Senior architecting leaders must start by addressing the "what" question. They provide the strategic commitment to innovation and set priorities. Because senior leaders have final responsibility for the results of innovation, it falls to them to ensure that all the projects in the innovation portfolio— whether conducted internally or externally—are aimed at critical priorities. They start by overseeing a rigorous exploration of the organization's needs and shaping the priorities for innovation so that resources can be allocated accordingly. They then determine how resources are allocated across the horizons, from 10 percent projects out to 10x ones at the furthest one. Additionally, they broadly shape priorities about problems and solutions within the three zones.

The role of senior leaders isn't over when the strategy has been defined and the portfolio allocation determined. Ideally, after they "step up" to set the strategic direction, they "step back" to allow their staff to deliver the innovation portfolio against these priorities, as our colleague Elsbeth Johnson advises.[3] In reality, as for most essential programs and activities, they will need to check on progress regularly. They cannot disappear and hope for the best.

Because innovation can take surprising turns, senior leaders will want to revisit the portfolio perspective on a regular cadence (perhaps every quarter) and dig into the detailed portfolio (say annually), though the high-level strategic priorities should remain stable for more than one year (unless there are truly unexpected events). These leaders will also want to retain some discretion so as to have flexibility in the face of unexpected opportunities (so long as they can also decide what to stop!). By assessing internal and external progress in a quarterly rhythm, they can stay alert to the changing innovation landscape.

Once the cadence for revisiting the portfolio is set, the portfolio itself becomes a management tool. Senior leaders will decide when to identify and fill gaps that have emerged and reallocate resources (likely annually). Meanwhile, other leaders in the organization can use the portfolio to see what the innovation teams are doing, which helps build support among the BAU senior leaders—essential for pull-through—and alignment for short- and long-term priorities.

Turning to the enabling middle managers in your organization, they are the people who must articulate your senior leadership's decisions into the defined projects in the portfolio. In other words, they ensure that your strategy is executed. Their power also comes from the portfolio: it's a framework they can use to cut through the complexity and confusion in the ecosystem (and internally) to ensure that the organization stays focused on its priorities.

Enabling leaders are typically the middle managers who run innovation units such as a corporate venture fund, an internal innovation lab, or the relationships with universities. They often manage many frontline entrepreneurial leaders and between them oversee a collection of the organization's ecosystem-facing activities as well as key investment-related activities focused on early-stage venture building and investing. They should have sufficient rank and experience to be able to advise you about the resources necessary to execute the strategy and the tactics for doing so. They should also have close enough relationships with you and other senior leaders to engage you when they need support and oversight.

Unlike senior leaders, middle managers will be responsible for only part of the innovation portfolio that is delivering on the leader's priorities. They might be focused on a particular zone, such as the PN zone, where business unit leaders typically work on new business opportunities or government mission leads address new challenges to be solved. In the SN zone, it is likely to be R&D managers focused on particular business and capability challenges, or accelerator leaders focused on a particular set of challenges. And in the N^2 zone, middle managers are often in the corporate venture fund (or government strategic innovation fund)—with their role in middle versus senior management likely determined by the size of the fund and scale of your organization. They might also be running an accelerator. In other organizations, we have found it fruitful to have middle managers organized by technical theme, for example, quantum, AI, novel materials. This is useful when you need to search across a wide range of possible zones in a technical domain.

Regardless of how portfolio responsibilities are allocated, the problem/ solution matrix we introduced in chapter 2 is also an important managerial tool for middle managers. It illustrates the innovation portfolio in more granular detail than senior leaders probably need to use (except on an annual basis), and it can be regularly updated (probably quarterly) to account for the internal *stage-gate* process. This is where projects gather more resources (so the bubbles increase in size), some are killed, and others from the internal system and external ecosystem are introduced (figure 5.2).

As a senior leader, a key role is to provide budget clarity and consistency to your middle managers. To fully empower them, you can provide them with flexibility to reallocate budgets when innovation cycles show that some projects are doing well, and others aren't, so that they are not bogged down in bureaucracy when they want to move projects along or kill others. Working within their own part of the portfolio, middle managers will therefore have an opportunity to prune their elements of the portfolio (probably quarterly) in close collaboration with their frontline teams.

We find it useful to recognize that middle managers may not always have previous experience as innovators or have been rewarded for undertaking

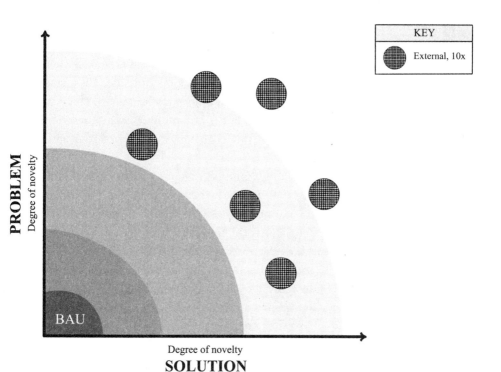

Figure 5.2
Projects in the external ecosystem out at the further (e.g., 10x) horizon.

high-risk initiatives. In earlier roles, innovation may have seemed to them (or their staff) to be a distraction from operational excellence in BAU and delivery of their targets. Indeed, in many organizations, such mid-level leaders are seen as the "frozen middle," where initiatives from above—and especially from below—stall (or freeze!). In our experience, however, these middle-management leaders are rational actors: for them to rally, and take risks, they must see that leaders above them are indeed committed to innovation, not just at the level of innovation theater but through priorities and resources. And the best way for you to demonstrate this is with clear budget authority and prioritization—not necessarily with the largest budgets but rather the clearest sense of priorities (and the underlying rationale driving those decisions).

Empowering middle managers is essential. Beyond funding, your middle managers will need access to resources including, though not limited to, internal expertise, infrastructure, and access to customer relationships to be effective in delivering on their part of the ecosystem portfolio. Sometimes you will need to help them access such resources from elsewhere in the organization. But collective decision-making and shared resources across the portfolio is what will ultimately deliver on your goals. This is an important role for middle managers but is not always easy in a resource-constrained environment. As such, it is a behavior that senior leaders must encourage and support.

Without senior leaders taking a portfolio view across the entire problem/solution matrix, individual middle managers run the risk of leaving whitespace unexplored, of adding duplication, or of fragmenting innovation ecosystem engagement efforts. More than simply the sum of activities, the portfolio reveals how these managers can work together to derive the benefits of internal and external innovation. In Jaguar Land Rover, for example, there was a lead ecosystem orchestrator (serving at a level close to senior leadership) who gathered middle managers across a range of ecosystem-facing roles. In other organizations, the middle-management group for external engagement regularly comes together to compare their efforts and their insights, in a sort of innovation committee or working-level governance board. Without this coordination (rather than necessarily control), efforts might be unnecessarily duplicative and wasteful. This should include senior leaders on a reasonable cadence for information and support, and serve as a platform for making strategic asks to senior leaders.

Finally, there is an ongoing role for you as a senior leader in serving as the advocate for your middle managers across other parts of the wider organization. Belinda has had to do this repeatedly when other parts of the organization are asking for rapid results or want to keep shifting priorities. Mike at MassMutual found it critical to encourage managers to collaborate to ensure that the ecosystem efforts in the portfolio were effectively linked to internal projects and that learning was transferred from external projects to internal ones. This higher-order support ensures that your ecosystem engagement delivers on your priorities.

To turn the tables, what should middle management be asking of you—their senior leaders—so that they can enable your organizational priorities? What should Abby be asking of Belinda so that she can be truly effective at meeting Belinda's goals? What we have heard from these (oft-beleaguered) middle managers is the following: provide us with clear headcount and support for our innovation teams. Allow us some flexibility in the allocation and especially reallocation of resources if projects don't work as expected. Please don't be surprised if we don't always select the more "usual suspects" in the organization for entrepreneurial roles (more on this below). Show a genuine interest in what we are learning from the innovation ecosystem, but please don't expect immediate results. We will provide insights on a regular basis, and some of them are truly exciting!

We would be remiss if we left this section on the "what" without outlining the essential role played by entrepreneurial leaders on the front line, both out in the ecosystem and inside your innovation system. With their focus on innovation projects day in and day out, they will be able to provide critical input about how specific projects are going. Their updates about key projects will be insightful as they are closest to the realities of the innovation work, and their voices should shape the conversation about priorities and specific projects in the portfolio. They should also be empowered to raise concerns with their middle managers when they observe that the organization is not getting what it needs from its engagements—and be sufficiently supported when they do.

In turn, middle management needs to support frontline leaders. When Abby took on a middle-management role for Belinda, she spent much of her time clarifying and restructuring the work of her frontline team. It was clear to her that without these internal entrepreneurs, engagement interactions would not bear fruit in the long run: as we have discussed, ecosystem engagement requires ongoing commitment and a willingness and ability to move rapidly when entrepreneurs need support and resources. Your frontline employees are the ones who will have, ideally, the trusted relationships they need externally in the ecosystem and internally in the organization to ask for the resources they need to be effective. The same goes for your entrepreneurial leaders.

Identifying the Whitespace

Your innovation priorities and the portfolio that you build to deliver on them is your "best guess" at the projects you need to deliver to achieve your goals. But innovation is, as we have noted from the start, subject to significant risk. There is also great uncertainty—outcomes that cannot even be imagined, let alone defined. And innovation ecosystems are often where these future outcomes are being imagined and realized, and where they are being developed at the horizon. The events and insights at this evolving innovation horizon will ultimately fill the *whitespace* in your portfolio.

It is important to regularly leave time and resources to adapt to unexpected insights coming from the innovation ecosystem to maximize the returns from your ecosystem engagements. When done well, following the approaches we have laid out, being in the ecosystem can shape our understanding of wider innovation trends and patterns. And yet in their rush to work on projects, frontline team members often forget (or are not given an opportunity) to feed their insights back to the middle managers who lead portfolio activities, and then up to you as you make strategic prioritization decisions. And as such, your portfolio is too static and not sufficiently adaptive—not to fads and fashions but to truly meaningful changes happening at great speed.

Entrepreneurial leaders are likely to be the best scouts and partners in the ecosystem to identify new and unexpected trends in emerging technologies or new markets. They should be briefed about the internal priorities and problems the organization has decided to address, allowing them to identify opportunities that meet the spirit of the priorities, not simply the letter of the strategic "shopping list." They will also be well placed to overcome blind spots because they understand the big picture. Conversely, they will know the value that the organization can bring to its partners.

Making time for insights to be brought into the organization by your talented frontline staff from the whitespace of the problem/solution matrix will more than pay back the incremental time it takes. And by doing this process of feeding back insights, as well as project updates, you will continue to energize your middle managers. Last, the work of addressing whitespace and managing the innovation portfolio together will ensure that your high-level priorities are aligned with the reality of the innovation horizon.

Leading for the "Who": Selecting the Right People to Lead for Innovation

A senior leader in a large tech company—one of our former students—surprised our class on a recent visit when she told them that she spent over 20 percent of her time on people management: asking the question of "who" should be driving priorities and in what role.

To help you be more strategic in your choice of "who," we have spent a significant amount of time examining the characteristics of those people and the roles that make for successful innovation leaders at every level. And we have learned a lot about the characteristics of successful employees who can deliver on your innovation ecosystem engagement plans and drive your priorities for innovation forward. We have discovered three important aspects of these choices.

First, more than specific narrow skill sets, these roles need commitment from the individuals and career paths from the organization. Second, the type of talent you are looking for to represent your organization in the ecosystem will vary for front line versus middle management—and by which zone in the portfolio and stage of the innovation cycle. Last, we recognize that as senior leaders, it will fall to you, at times, to represent your organization in the external innovation ecosystem. While you should do this sparingly as you have a wide range of other responsibilities, your visible commitment amplifies your ability to hire and retain talent for your ecosystem engagement.

We outline these three elements in turn.

Committed Individuals, with Clear Career Paths

Who you select to become an enabling middle manager or entrepreneurial staff member on the front lines of the ecosystem will depend on various factors. The expertise, experience, networks, and cultural fit of each individual should be aligned with the priorities in the innovation portfolio that they are responsible for. But equally important is their interest and curiosity about the cast of other ecosystem characters—entrepreneurs, universities, or risk capital providers—with whom they will work to deliver your portfolio goals. This is not to say that they need to "look the part" or have the same demographics. But having a respect for, interest in, and at times experience of these other stakeholder groups can be particularly powerful.

For Belinda, as we noted, one of the most successful middle managers working with start-ups in the ecosystem was Abby—a longtime career government official with a keen sense of the excitement of entrepreneurship (her parents had run a small business) and an intensity that could match that of the founders she engaged. She also had the curiosity to serve as a sounding board to both founders and internal teams seeking meaningful engagement with the outside teams that Abby's group of frontline tech scouts were discovering. This helped her to build strong relationships that could then translate into deeper interactions when start-ups had completed an experimental cycle and were ready to participate in a departmental challenge, pilots/trials, or later a contract.

Finding people like Abby takes time. Often, a senior executive, when they wish to task someone to initiate contact in the ecosystem, simply finds an employee who happens to be available during a busy time or is enthusiastic about the opportunity. But ad hoc choices may lead to people who do not have the necessary skills, or come from the wrong place in the organization, who are then poorly placed to be able to follow through. This is a mistake: it is worth finding the right talent so that your ecosystem engagements succeed internally and externally.

Today's modern career paths will likely make your job of finding the right people for ecosystem engagement more challenging. As career progression has become increasingly flexible, and people move jobs more frequently, those inclined toward ecosystem roles—connecting to entrepreneurs, risk capital, or university researchers—tend to match their interests by working directly in those organizations. (This concentration of specialized talent is part of the benefit of ecosystem engagement in the first place!). But the flip side of the flight of talent into ecosystems is that aspiring leaders in you organization may be less interested in careers solely within large public or private sector organizations and might find an ecosystem-facing role appealing.

Your role as a senior leader will therefore be to identify and build up an internal bench of talented frontline staff and middle managers who know your organization well, appreciate your organization's strategy and priorities, and are interested in translating them into external relationships and projects. They need to be dedicated to an ecosystem role as part of their career progression and willing to roll up their sleeves to live and breathe the ecosystem for a period.

As you find and nurture this internal talent, we advise you to ensure that innovation ecosystem roles for middle and frontline innovation leaders are on a successful career path within your organization. In the past, some of these ecosystem roles—corporate-university liaison positions or external tech scouting—were seen as dead ends or soon-to-retire types of roles. Or they might be perceived as too far from senior leadership attention and out of the line of sight when it comes to promotion opportunities. If these beliefs (or the reality) persist, then your ability to recruit great people to deliver on the ecosystem portfolio will fall flat. Instead, it is worth integrating external ecosystem-facing roles into more traditional internally focused career progression so you build a group of people with both internal insights and external credibility.

Now let us turn to selecting the right individuals to drive your strategy forward.

Selecting the Right Entrepreneurial and Enabling Leaders

Your portfolio can guide choices of middle-management and frontline entrepreneurial leaders. As we outlined in chapters 2 and 3, the portfolio describes the gaps you need to fill—the key problems, and the technologies that may provide solutions—as well as the stakeholders who are likely to help you fill them, that is, the people whom your frontline team will be engaging.

You, and the middle managers, who select your entrepreneurial staff need to recognize that external ecosystem interactions are most effectively led by individuals who have had some experience on both sides of BAU, that is, in your mission-facing or business-focusing groups, as well as with the innovation engines within your organization, such as R&D and capabilities. New hires typically find it harder to undertake such a delicate, externally facing role early in their time at your organization.

Counterintuitively, it is not often the staff from teams at the far ends of the innovation process—either from early-stage R&D units or from later-stage M&A teams—who are best suited for these roles. Both of these extremes may have deep knowledge of the current research, business, or acquirable ventures, but they can also have quite a narrow perspective on what else the organization is looking for and who are the most effective innovators. The ideal ones for engaging the diverse array of external stakeholders more often inhabit the space between research and acquisition.

The entrepreneurial leaders who are most effective as ecosystem engagers are often themselves innovators but with a sense of structure and organization to enable integration with internal work: that is, they must be able to be operate outside the organization without going rogue (and forgetting the priorities of you, their employer). To guide you as you seek out the right internal talent, we outline some of the characteristics of these staff according to the zone in the portfolio for which they are responsible. We have found it most helpful to provide *personas* to shape your hiring choices rather than a list of attributes.

Engaging the ecosystem in the PN zone entails searching for solutions to problem-novelty and specialized resources—especially talent—to meet your customers' new needs or an emerging, messy mission problem. This means hiring team members who really understand the customer or mission challenge they are charged with solving. In public sector delivery organizations, they should ideally have experience with the mission or be respected by those internal mission leaders. When it comes to the private sector, it is helpful to select people with insights into your existing customers but interest in new lines of business. Beyond this internal connectivity, you will wish to seek individuals who are excited about new, digital technologies that are likely to be the sorts of solutions that you will be seeking.

For Kristo, this meant bringing across a civilian staff member—Kaarel—who had worked in his defense ministry and who was young but well regarded by the serving officers who respected his work ethic, his interest in their challenges, and his willingness to always roll up his sleeves and solve their problems in a new and creative way. By hiring Kaarel into the newly formed innovation hub, Kristo knew he would have someone who could bridge the gap between the internal problem owners and the external digital start-ups—especially those at the earliest phases of their innovation cycles.

Large organizations whose priorities lie in exploring the SN zone will need to consider who to hire on the front line to explore novel technology areas at low TRLs, in universities, and, increasingly, from some very early-stage start-up ventures—often spinning out of universities. For Eni, the Italian energy giant, this meant selecting people who could come and spend time on MIT's campus as part of the MIT Energy Initiative and at the PSFC. Obviously, a technical background was essential—not necessarily someone with a PhD in plasma physics but one who could engage with the team of research scientists, postdocs, and doctoral students. This sort of role, when part of a strategic university engagement, is increasingly sought after by young ambitious R&D team members who want to get exposed to the innovation horizon while also being able to bring ideas back into your organization.

Finally, in the N^2 zone, Abby was just the sort of person Belinda needed and has a profile you might also find interesting: someone with an ambitious, fast-paced approach, committed to the organization and liked by mission owners. Abby in turn had to find people to go out into the ecosystem and back into the building to match novel solutions to the emerging new problem sets. The people she selected did not have to be the most technical but be willing to dig into new trends in areas like AI or quantum. They might have demonstrated this by taking online courses or executive programs, or simply by reading and talking to people. But they also needed to be intrigued by the start-up entrepreneurial journey so that they could understand and communicate with entrepreneurial teams, especially those leading deep-tech IDEs.

Belinda also needed someone with deeper financial skills at the middle-management level who could interact with the VC community, not just entrepreneurs on a one-on-one basis. And this is repeated when large organizations—public and private sector—set up venture units and especially develop their focus on CVCs and SIFs. This sort of middle manager and their frontline staff members are more akin to partners and associates at a VC firm, interested in looking across the pipeline of start-up opportunities, doing deep dives into the ventures, and connecting to their VC counterparts. A deep skill set in finance would be useful but was hard for Belinda to find in the government sector. Instead, she sought people who had spent time in finance but gave it up for a more mission-driven public sector career. In this way, their prior expertise could be leveraged for the good of the organization's public goals. Indeed, in our experience, we have found that those who excel as the mid-level enabling leaders are often close to the business or to mission customers, quick to take the initiative, and well-connected internally. If they are convinced that this opportunity is "career-enhancing," they will likely jump at it to play an ecosystem-facing role.

A final note on the type of people you choose to serve in key innovation roles: they must be able to work externally and also build links and relationships internally. This means championing their innovation efforts within the organization and building connections to key business units or internal customers, creating a demand later in the innovation process to "pull through" external innovations. The uncertainty of this process and the challenge of innovation can drive you to hire people who are familiar to the organization and will fit in, who are similar, or who have similar interests. But we know that innovation clearly benefits from diversity—of perspective, background, creativity, and other dimensions. It can lead to an exploration of a range of diverse problem/solution matches that the

BAU might not think of. The power of senior leaders is to build innovation teams across their organizations who balance internal experience and the ability to integrate external innovation, with distinctive, new voices who share new insights in new ways.

Engaging the External Ecosystem
The leaders heading out into the ecosystem must not forget that they are representatives of your organization, and so they need to have sufficient experience and status internally to represent the organization externally. As you build up your team of frontline ecosystem-facing staff and of essential middle managers to lead on specific parts of the portfolio—such as hackathons and prizes, an accelerator, or corporate venture fund—it is important to return to the question of "who" goes out from the organization into the ecosystem from each level.

At the top of the leadership pyramid, senior leaders set the strategic direction for the large organization's ecosystem engagement. As such, they may be best placed to have occasional meetings with the most senior risk capital players (like the experienced GPs at a VC fund), and some senior professors and administrators at the university, to develop more strategic high-level relationships that cover a range of activities. It can also be useful for your organization for senior leaders to interact with some of the more mature start-up ventures that are reaching the acceleration or scaling stages, and where more significant partnerships could make a difference for them and for your organization.

Your enabling middle managers might best be deployed to engage with the frontline GPs at risk capital VCs, as they have a closer perspective of particular (business) problems and (technical) solutions. They will also find it helpful to engage with leaders of external hackathons and accelerators, and those who run venture studios that are a source of potential ideas and projects at the various cycles of maturity. Of course, one should not forget the power of others with technical and market expertise who often sit in the middle of the organization. Middle managers may wish to draw on expertise from their colleagues across their own level of the organization, especially those whose experience could be invaluable to entrepreneurs, to professors and others in the university, and to some of those in VC funds for whom your organization might later be an essential partner (on their most promising portfolio companies).

Last, at the base of the pyramid are the entrepreneurial leaders who execute the engagement strategy and deliver frontline innovation outcomes. They could usefully engage with student founders at the university and become integrated into student-facing activities and events. They are also ideal to connect directly to early-stage entrepreneurs. Similarly, they can engage deeply with entrepreneurs at accelerators, serving as mentors, attending events, and integrating into the community. They might also get to know the wider community of associates at VC firms who gather at investment summits and other such activities.

Without being overly prescriptive, when we look across organizations building an effective ecosystem engagement approach that yields important outcomes and have the impact that the leadership desires, we find several useful rules of thumb as follows:

- If the primary focus is the university stakeholder, perhaps some senior professors, then an equally senior or relevantly technical person from the large organization might be appropriate. If the target of the university engagement is early-stage start-up entrepreneurs (including student spinouts from the university), then it might be an equivalently young or entrepreneurial leader from the organization.

- If the target for engagement is the risk capital stakeholder, then a variety of the large organization's staff might be appropriate. If it is the VC-investing GPs who need engaging, then a less senior (perhaps enabling middle management) representative may be more appropriate, with more junior staff engaging the junior VC associates themselves.

- If the focus is on later-stage entrepreneurs, especially start-ups in the scaling cycle or beyond, then the venture-funding units of the large organizations, or a corporate's M&A team, might be the right people to engage them. Another target might be the heads of portfolio companies in portfolios run by a risk capital fund.

Leading for the "How": Innovating through a Phased Process

With the necessary direction, sufficient resources, and the right leaders at each level, your organization is in a position for you to decide how best to structure your engagement with the ecosystem. Of course, we have already covered this topic in detail in chapter 4, but here we want to return to a series of organizational issues that frequently beset senior, middle, and frontline leaders as they try and make the most of their innovation ecosystem engagements.

Four issues frustrate senior leaders and often drive their innovation system and ecosystem activities to fail to deliver: fragmented engagement, lack of internal/external integration, limited pull-through (including the ability to kill projects), and poor measurement. We look at each one in turn.

Fragmented Engagement across the Ecosystem Cycles

Decisions about how to engage the ecosystem should be led by your trusted group of innovation-focused middle managers, who present the key options to senior leadership for endorsement. This approach ensures strong and visible support from the top.

As choices of engagement stage and mode (the "how") are made, you must be clear about what each modality will bring back into the organization. We repeat the following graphic (of "programs" matching the innovation "cycles" in the external ecosystem) as a reminder to guide engagement and the overall benefits of each type of interaction (figure 5.3).

The challenge for middle managers is to make the choices by cycle and program even though many of these sorts of ecosystem activities are not

	Exploring	Validating	Accelerating	Scaling
Programs	Hackathons & Bootcamps	Competitions & Venue Studios	Accelerators	Venture Funds
Program (& Other) Funding	Small prizes, Small awards, some friends, & family money	Grants and awards (can range up to large $$$), small equity investments	SAFEs or early equity, as well as prizes (for success in accelerator) or grants	Equity Series A, B, etc. from investors & some Work Programs (from government)

Figure 5.3
Large organizations must choose the right innovation "cycle."

ones in which they have participated and which they might have only read about in the newspaper or in innovation blogs. It is the role of entrepreneurial frontline teams to suggest how and where to engage, and then for middle managers to shape these choices into a set of plans for interaction that balance focus with fragmentation.

Your choices will depend on your best assessment of the gaps in your portfolio the zone where the problem/solution match lies, and which ecosystem stakeholders likely have the novel ideas you need, the specialized resources, or the approach to experimentation. Recall our discussion in chapter 4:

- If the priority is in the PN zone, and if you think the solution space is quite mature, then a series of hackathons may well reveal novel early-stage ideas that can be adapted. You will also want to engage start-up teams at a slightly later innovation cycle through challenges inspired by your mission problems or your customer insights. Last, with a clear set of challenges, you may choose to make a long-term commitment to an accelerator program partnership (like MassMutual has done with MassChallenge).

- If your priorities are in the SN zone, you will likely want to interact with universities, but less through sponsored research, and perhaps more through proactive approaches, such as reverse-pitching competitions or engaging the spinout ventures from the labs. You may also want to interact with deep-tech start-ups, particularly technical fields. For this, an accelerator might be useful as well, as some large corporates have found with Startup Autobahn or with the entrepreneurship activities at TUM.

- If the focus is on the N^2 zone, you will probably want to connect informally with the ecosystem to explore whitespace while developing a venture studio, a CVC, or a network of risk capital relationships. This is similar to what J&J has done with its extensive set of activities across geographies and types of innovation, or as Saudi Aramco is doing with the transformation of its energy business to consider sustainability and renewable resources.

Ecosystem engagement, as our list suggests, is grounded in an (often extensive) collection of activities and programs, from hackathons and bootcamps to CVC and cocreation. That said, there is a benefit to regularly bringing these activities and the participants together to ensure the whole is greater than the sum of its parts. Coherence across the efforts also requires a clear message on how each of these activities is different and provides unique access for innovators, not complex duplication.

Even if each program is carefully curated, there are likely to be overlaps and quite possibly opportunities for confusion in the ecosystem about your organization's intent. For middle managers working internally with their senior sponsors, designing external ecosystem engagement also requires understanding the individual elements of the ecosystem activities and knowing how to bring them together in useful groupings—whether that is across cycles for a given zone or across similar solutions. For example, it is important to ensure that projects that emerge from, for example, a prize challenge can be linked to a subsequent accelerator program and ultimately be pursued with an investment if it continues to support your organizational priorities. Too often, projects fall through the cracks between cycles, and opportunities for strategic value are lost. Making this logic clear internally reduces internal fragmentation and external confusion.

For example, the US Department of Defense now has dozens of outward-facing ecosystem engagement units, pioneered by the DIU and the Defense Innovation Board. Teams across the Pentagon now design units to address a "what" question—and then to plan and execute (the "who" and "how")—but separately at the tactical level. The innovation benefit to a large organization like this is amplified when someone senior gets a sense (perhaps from a central innovation team) of how they fit into a portfolio, avoiding fragmentation and unplanned duplication. That team can then also help such units engage with one another so they triage promising projects, help manage handovers between units, and generally guide external partners as they move from one unit to another along the pipeline. At J&J and Standard Bank (mentioned earlier), the companies regularly convene their ecosystem leaders to ensure that the individual programs collectively deliver shared value and insight and to craft a unified message for the innovation ecosystem. Small central teams can support the innovation efforts in large organizations, to reduce both fragmentation and duplication, while helping senior leaders ensure that innovation leads to meaningful impact.

Lack of External/Internal Integration

If external efforts seem fragmented or fractured, then so too is the fault line between internal and external efforts. The alignment between ecosystem innovation cycles and the stages in your innovation pipeline is a chance to overcome this. It will also ensure that external efforts guide your internal projects (and vice versa) rather than competing with them.

To make the most of ecosystem engagement projects, leaders at all three levels need to monitor the full set of external programs, ensure their efforts are coordinated, and share their insights with leaders of the internal portfolio on a timely basis. On a tactical level, middle managers must connect internal and external efforts in different parts of the portfolio in various ways:

- Offering opportunities for individuals from within the organization to work on ecosystem activities as mentors, judges, and experts, as Mass-Mutual did
- Sharing specialized infrastructure and experimentation facilities as BHP has done
- Sharing attention by incorporating internal and external projects into pitch days, competitions, and other internal innovation stages
- Pooling activities, for example, having common resources that both external and internal projects bid into for future work, such as MIT/USAF AI Accelerator's joint research

While ensuring that their managers do the hard work of engaging innovators and entrepreneurs externally, senior leaders must also shape strategic conversations around how these external activities complement internal ones and what is learned across the piece. They can help ensure that middle managers cocreate the ways in which their external portfolio connects. These middle managers will understand their internal system well, while the entrepreneurial leaders will know the external stakeholders better. Together, they will be able to identify options for interaction with the internal portfolio that should satisfy both sides.

The ask is that you, as a senior leader, hold both internal and external innovation efforts accountable against the organization's priorities. It is ultimately the responsibility of those at the top to clearly identify how particular organizational decisions—of internal process and external ecosystem interaction—will support their overarching innovation priorities, especially those out at the more distant innovation horizon.

Additionally, senior leaders must ensure that their middle managers who are driving internal innovation do not allow a "not invented here" syndrome to dominate internal processes, thus starving the external projects of resources or rendering them less effective. Senior leaders can support this shift in perspective by designing how their external activities connect to internal processes. Here, the internal innovation processes are essential: they set the internal tempo, the criteria, and the filters for each stage of the innovation portfolio. They are where choices are made and, ideally, where resources are allocated.

Achieving *Pull-Through* of Ecosystem Innovation

Even if internal and external projects are managed in an integrated fashion in their early innovation cycles, challenges with the innovation pipeline continue. Many organizations can identify and resource many small projects at stage 1 of the innovation pipeline or in cycle 1 within the external innovation ecosystem.

The difficulty arises at the later stage gates or milestones. This is a moment to make clear decisions as to which projects should be stopped and which deserve to continue and be allocated more significant resources to allow them to complete experiments for stage 2 and especially at stage 3, the accelerating phase, when there are much greater resources needed to reduce key risks. As we have noted in chapter 4, this moment of external evaluation happens in the harsh reality of the innovation ecosystem.

Inside organizations, it is difficult to decisively kill projects, just as it is challenging to allocate additional, larger-scale resources—money, people, access to infrastructure—to projects, especially in finding specialized people who are in high demand, not just those who are available. Instead, we often observe projects that continue with the same limited amounts of resources, ultimately making it hard for them to succeed at scale. This problem may happen at different stages in your organization. For example, for Kristo, the problem was always the final scaling from stage 3 to 4 when projects needed to shift to a large-scale government contract. For our colleagues at MiningCorp, their challenge was stage 2 to 3 when their projects confronted regulatory issues within a real operational context and thus stalling in their attempts at acceleration.

We have observed the same pattern of limited pull-through for innovation ecosystem projects when large organizations nurture external projects in, for example, an accelerator but then fail to have the organizational ability to pull them through with additional resources and perhaps more internal integration.

When used in a way that is inspired by the external ecosystem, the pipeline's gate aligns with the ecosystem's cycles and milestones, providing opportunities for the pull-through of activities from the ecosystem, or stopping projects. These efforts are often best done through the comparison of internal and external projects at the same stage in the innovation journey, with the selection of the most effective project to move ahead based on the limited resources available to scaling.

For each project, at each stage, senior leaders should ask their middle managers the following questions:

- Does this sort of **novelty** still fit with our portfolio? And is it the best project to solve our problem or explore this kind of solution? If not, does it make sense to stop the project? (This might not mean that the project dies, as it may fit elsewhere, but the current team may come to the end of its shared journey).

- If it is to proceed, what **specialized resources** are needed to power the next innovation phase? How much money? What time and talent? Should we find it internally or externally?

- What **experimentation** infrastructure is needed for the technical, customer, scale-up, and regulatory pathways? Where will these resources come from? Which business or capability units?

In turn, middle managers will ask their frontline entrepreneurial leaders the following questions, the answers to which the senior leaders will use to make decisions:

- Do we want to bring the project fully in-house? Or should we keep the project external but provide some support while "co-investing" with others? And if so, what form will that support take? Will it be a customer contract, an equity investment, or some other resource?

- Who will orchestrate that journey internally so that the external team on the innovation project continues to wish to engage with us? Is it the entrepreneurial leader or a new internal champion?

The transition between phases is a dangerous moment in the lives of innovation projects, when a lack of speed, understanding, or commitment can change the nature of relationships or undermine effective ecosystem engagement. (This is true of stages for internal projects, but it is especially fraught for external stakeholders in innovation cycles, for whom the

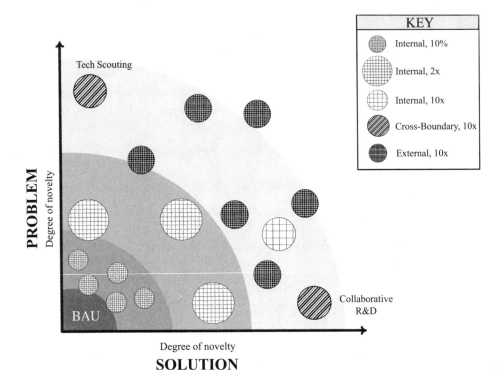

Figure 5.4
Mapping external innovation to the internal portfolio, to fill in gaps.

internal organization is often a labyrinth.) It is here that taking a systematic approach pays dividends. This approach reduces the risk that the internal system will create antibodies against the external project and reject the transplanted idea.

Effective pull-through is best viewed through the prism of the problem/solution matrix. When the internal efforts at innovation are mapped against those innovations in the external ecosystem, it is possible to see which of the latter usefully fills a gap in the internal effort and should be prioritized for pull-through (see figure 5.4).

In some ways, moving to the next stage/cycle might be a potentially rewarding decision. But is it rewarded equally if it is internal versus external in origin? Or does a "not invented here" approach mean that rewards are reduced if internal projects are killed? Are there rewards and visibility for projects that continue externally (if that is their most effective home)? And most important, are there rewards to killing something to free up resources, or is this labeled as failure?

The answers to these questions can be the difference between a successful program of innovation ecosystem engagement and a suboptimal one (and potentially career-limiting for many of your middle managers). For senior leaders, you have the opportunity to shift the answers to these questions if you can shape the nature of the pipeline and its evaluation processes in productive ways that allow for internal and external pull-through. If you cannot make these changes, then the efforts at strategic prioritization and tactical approaches to innovation will not provide your anticipated return on investment.

Measuring and Communicating Engagement, and System-Wide Impact

Our final element of "how" is measurement. As in any successful organization, leaders must have clear, consistent, and aligned goals; success criteria; and a timescale for engaging the ecosystem. They should use the same metrics to measure the progress and results of every ecosystem engagement. These metrics must align with the organization's internal innovation metrics so that every project's performance can be understood in the same terms. Problems arise when ecosystem engagement is held to a higher standard than internal projects or when it is not measured at all.

A dashboard of ecosystem engagements can provide each level of leadership with the data it needs to make decisions. Entrepreneurial leaders' key metrics on the front line include program-by-program facts and figures, such as the number of start-ups applying and number selected. For investments or working with investors, the metrics might be similar—number of investments seen and number selected. For middle managers, these metrics must aggregate across activities so that they have a complete view of the projects in their domain. They might also consider a series of additional metrics depending on the innovation cycles that they are most extensively engaged with in the ecosystem:

- the diversity of technologies they are exploring,
- the diversity of people involved in their engagements (see the previous sidebar on bias in innovation and entrepreneurship),
- unexpected insights, and
- the innovation cycle of each project.

For senior leaders, a key question is timing: when should performance be reported? Smart senior leaders will create metrics that track inputs (such as budget, people, and time) as well as intermediate outputs (such as an experiment's result, or the creation of a prototype). They might also capture progress—in line with a *logic model*—toward the *outputs* or possibly even the ultimate *outcomes* that matter to the business (such as new revenue) or mission (such as new capabilities), delivered in a timely fashion.

Warning: We know that some engagements, particularly those 10x projects on the most distant horizon of novel problems and solutions, will take more time. Leaders should be realistic and not disappointed that these efforts are not yielding results at the same rate as others that are closer to the 10 percent innovation horizon.

Pulling together the leadership challenges that come with driving strategic innovation ecosystem engagement makes it clear that the task of building and delivering on an internal and external innovation portfolio is not simple. There are roles for leaders at the most senior level in the organization, but they rely on their middle managers to enable their strategic goals and, in turn, depend on frontline entrepreneurial leaders to bring fresh perspectives, energy, and drive to their projects.

For each level in the organization, there is much to be done to clarify the "what" of ecosystem engagement—what must be done and to what purpose. Each level of leadership will answer the question of what their role is differently. That said, senior leaders must provide an overarching vision of their priorities so that in the rapidly changing innovation landscape, middle and frontline teams can respond in real time.

Given that the work of innovation is about validating risks and then experimenting to learn and evaluate, the need for autonomy (and speed) is high. This means that answering the "who" question—who will lead these efforts well at every level—is essential. The task of innovation is not routine and repetitive. This does not mean it has to be messy, unstructured, and entirely bottom-up, but it does mean that a slow top-down bureaucracy will be unlikely to succeed. As such, the quality and commitment of your middle and entrepreneurial leaders matters. They may not have the skill sets and credentials of those in the ecosystem in start-ups, universities, and risk capital, but their willingness to engage with these stakeholders on behalf of your organization's goals is essential.

Last, when it comes to "how," we recognize that the design of ecosystem engagements is only the start. These efforts fail if they are fragmented, do not manage the internal-external tensions, and will not yield benefits if leaders at all levels cannot create the conditions for effective pull-through: killing some projects while increasing resources for others.

These are important and exciting challenges for leaders.

Key Points from Chapter 5: Leadership for Ecosystem Engagement

Having determined "how" your large organization will engage the ecosystem, it is important to address the leadership needed to make a success of this:

- Distributed leadership—with responsibility at multiple levels within the hierarchy—is generally more effective than command and control (especially for innovation).

- Nimble, innovation-oriented organizations need a three-level leadership pyramid:

  ○ Senior-level leaders play an "architecting" role, stepping up to set strategic direction, optimizing the internal system, and selecting the right people.

  ○ Middle-level leaders play an "enabling" role, translating strategic priorities into innovation activity that will complement traditional BAU.

  ○ Frontline leaders play an "entrepreneurial" role, both within their organization's system and in the external ecosystem.

The three levels of leaders use the portfolio (based on the problem/solution matrix), and its three zones, as a shared management tool for their individual efforts:

- Leading for the "what": setting priority targets, seeking those externally, and then being ready to "pull-through" the identified innovation

- Leading for the "who": selecting the right people to lead for innovation, engage the ecosystem, and then report back to the internal system

- Leading for the "how": innovating through a phased process and assessing innovation external cycles and how it can match internal stages

To achieve "pull-through," the measures for such ecosystem engagement should flow from the "what, who, and how" of your innovation strategy, with realistic time frames.

Turning to chapter 6, we will now look at the political and cultural challenges.

6 Political and Cultural Challenges

Dr. Barry Stein, chief clinical innovation officer with Hartford HealthCare (HHC), was in his office in downtown Hartford. From the outside, the space looked somewhat nondescript, but inside, it had been transformed to reflect the exciting innovation initiative that Barry had been leading for several years: a mandate from his CEO to use innovation as a lynchpin for HHC's commitment to transforming healthcare delivery for its patients. His office walls were still covered with the framed medical certificates that represented the many years of academic work that had seen him qualify as a physician in his native South Africa and then as an interventional radiologist in Boston's storied Massachusetts General Hospital.

Barry was confident in his strategy: driving deeper relationships with start-up ventures in several ecosystems working at the cutting edge of digital healthcare to drive improvements in scheduling operating room usage, to find new ways to leverage the massive amounts of confidential patient data, and to improve patient outcomes while maintaining privacy. However, the organization's ability to accelerate innovation was fragmented and somewhat siloed, making it hard to innovate at pace and especially challenging to adopt ideas at scale. It was fragmented, like many hospital systems, because data resided in so many different information systems and because different medical specialists had quite distinctive approaches to innovation—especially to developing and scaling new approaches to patient care. While innovation was in the DNA of the HHC, it was almost as if the culture of innovation followed the culture of medicine, where each medical expert was a master craftsperson taking their own approach. Even in Barry's own area of expertise in interventional radiology, it took time for innovations (e.g., in minimally invasive procedures) to be widely adopted from one physician to another. Beyond the structural issues, Barry recognized that healthcare systems were conservative and risk averse as a cultural matter given their focus on life-saving activities: clinicians often made life and death decisions for thousands of patients each year. They viewed change as risky and preferred to change things slowly, especially within clinical settings.

To reckon with these challenges, Barry decided to apply the *three lenses*. This framework, developed at MIT in the 1990s, has leaders examine the challenges and opportunities for their organizations from three perspectives: strategic design, political, and cultural.[1] Up to this point, we have focused on strategic design—giving you rational ways, supported by research, to answer the three critical questions for innovation ecosystem engagement.

But change, for whatever purpose, often fails, not only from poor strategic design but also due to political and cultural barriers. This chapter focuses on the latter two and shows you how to use them to advance your innovation activities. We also explain how to use them to understand the other stakeholders in the ecosystem.

First, a brief overview of all three lenses: strategic design, political, and cultural.

The strategic design lens helps you to see your organization through its priorities (the "what"), the arrangement of people who carry them out, and the processes to support them (indeed, the strategic lens guides the "what, who, and how" that we have discussed at length thus far). These elements combine into a system for running the organization, including the operating model, org chart, and budget processes. When an organization has new priorities, this ultrarational view illuminates how to change the various parts of the organization to fit them. For example, a shift in demand for a product may call for opening or closing a plant, hiring staff or laying them off, or developing a more efficient manufacturing process. For Barry at HHC, this meant implementing a clearer stage-gate decision process to evaluate potential innovations (including understanding both the clinical problem and the solution). This process allowed him to adapt legacy processes by which innovations were selected to receive resources, and ensured that teams had an agile process to adapt or stop projects when an experiment did not yield results.

In contrast, the political lens focuses on people as human beings who, as Aristotle observed, are "political": they compete with each other for resources and position. They have needs and wants—for recognition, respect, or other drivers. As the late biologist E. O. Wilson once said, the "real problem of humanity" is that "we have Paleolithic emotions, medieval institutions, and god-like technology."[2]

Individuals, with all their emotions, may be formally linked to one another through the design of the rational org chart, but they have a range of other affiliations that connect them in informal ways that facilitate collaboration and maybe even resource distribution (at times faster than through formal channels). Or they may have affiliations that create frictions, conflicts, and patterns of resourcing that are misaligned with the organization's goals. While this behavior can be fraught with competing or contradictory interests, it also may enable variety, as passionate people with different ideas pursue the resources they need to get things done.

In a hospital setting, these informal networks might include the relationships among physicians who trained together or who share similar specialties, for example, medicine versus surgery. Or perhaps it can be observed in the different networks among nurses, technicians, and doctors, which make it hard to adopt medical innovations that require more interdisciplinary teamwork, except in hospitals that have worked hard to break down barriers across different groups.

In organizations like conglomerate MiningCorp, we have observed these networks forming around geologists (especially those who have been in challenging parts of the world together) versus others, or in government agencies such as Kristo's, where groups might separate between those in (military) uniform and civilians. While not problematic itself, the power of the political networks that underpin informal human behaviors can—if not appreciated (e.g., through the political lens)—doom change efforts.

The third "culture" lens offers a view into the way "things are done around here."[3] It shows the organization as an organic institution imbued with symbolic frameworks of meaning, represented in artifacts, values, and routines that are grounded in history. Culture reflects the unwritten rules about how things get done, what success looks like, and what we believe about organizational motivations (even when they are unspoken). It is reflected in how people dress and who gets invited to meetings (what time the meetings are, who's punctual or late, and whether someone sits at the table or at the edge!).

Today, culture can be observed in norms around whether people have their cameras on for online meetings or if groups eat lunch in meetings. It might be manifest in when and how awards are selected and given, who has a designated parking spot, and a host of other daily practices that people don't think much about. In a hospital, culture shapes the expectations for how long the trainee doctors' workweek ought to be and whether and how training occurs—through intense questioning or gentle inquiry. It can even be observed in the symbolism of the white coat versus green operating room "scrubs" that signify different roles as much as they serve a rational, practical purpose.

As MIT Professor Ed Schein observed over thirty years ago, culture is likely to be the most difficult organizational attribute to observe and therefore change (though it is often more apparent to newcomers or visitors).[4] In fact, culture usually outlasts products, services, founders, leadership, and all physical attributes of the organization.

Innovation Efforts Viewed through the Political and Cultural Lenses

The existing political and cultural elements of your organization have been crucial to its past success. They create useful shortcuts for actions that today support the BAU aspects of your organization (even though at the start of your organization's history, there were probably some original innovations that got things started): not long ago, today's BAU aspects (such as using on-premise computer servers) may have been resisted as innovations, though they now appear as the "norm" (with the related cultural elements seen as culture as usual) to be protected against the next wave of innovation. But often, these political and cultural features get in the way of strategic change, including the sorts of change that innovation near the far horizons demands, if it is to be effective and not just theatric.

If your strategic approach to innovation leads to tension and resistance to change in your organization, applying the political and cultural lenses can be fruitful for understanding where the friction is coming from (maybe from the BAU teams, the innovation teams, or both) and how to diffuse it.

Looking through the "Political" Lens

The challenge with implementing innovation often has less to do with the solutions or the wealth of opportunities they provide and more with the interests of people, their emotions, and the institutions they inhabit. Without reckoning with this political dimension of the organization, a more

expansive innovation portfolio is unlikely to prosper, even if the technological solutions it might bring to your organization or your customer problems hold tremendous value—to the mission or to the bottom line.

Viewing innovation work through the "political" lens can enable savvy
leaders to see obstacles where they might not expect them if they just look
at the org chart. Equally, this lens might reveal paths of least resistance, outside the formal lines of the organization, through more informal networks
and unexpected allies in your journey.

These insights might be especially important for senior leaders and their
middle managers in the earliest stages of ecosystem engagement, where
the commitment is new, some staff are rationally wary, and even early
wins have not yet been achieved. The staff might be concerned that their
pet projects will be cut or the reputation of the organization will be dam-
aged. Working with potential allies—individuals you know well or who are
known to have power in your organization beyond their job title—can help
you make early progress by, for example, visibly supporting your activities
so that it's clear that reputational risks are being carefully considered. Alternatively, those who fear they have something to lose might be persuaded
by others with similar backgrounds or experiences that external engagement is a worthwhile experiment.

This is not to say that you should only deploy innovation in areas of
the business where you find people who are committed to it, or where you
have friends, as that approach is also risky. It can lead to distortions in
your portfolio of innovative activities that are only aligned with people you
know. Regardless, these networks must be confronted and used when possible. The key is to find allies who can support your interests and to identify
adversaries and find ways to bring them on board.

Sometimes it is wise—perhaps *politique*—to bring on board those who
are not enthused about a new problem but who are passionate about the
new solution to be deployed. These sorts of technology lovers can—if they
can be persuaded—become advocates for broader innovation activities if
they are first asked to share their expertise and perhaps asked to find the
solutions they like the best. Conversely, problem owners who are skepti-
cal about new solutions might be converted if they are asked to vet solutions, perhaps by serving as judges in a hackathon. (They might even have
resources in their business unit that could help with the innovation effort:
their early engagement will help with integrating innovation projects into

their business units later, as these projects cycle through stages of experimentation.) Such collaboration can help ensure that your innovation activities are supported through the journey to impact, so long as you maintain a clear focus on how these relationships support your long-term priorities.

At other times, the right people to engage might not only be those with relevant business or technical roles but also those who—for whatever reason—have stature, credibility, and influence within the organization. They can be revered experts, influential executives, folk heroes, or organizational curmudgeons. Politically savvy leaders will want to identify who these informal leaders are and get them on board while asking them to convert others to the cause.

The potential challenges of existing networks were something that Barry confronted in his new chief clinical innovation officer role. He found that the distinct social networks—and frankly tensions—that existed at times between clinicians on the one hand and other functional leaders on the other (e.g., IT, operations, supply chain) meant that innovation had traditionally been carried out just among physicians who learned informally from one another or through more structured (often slow) channels. Both had their limitations: clinicians could not scale their impact, while the administrators could not really change medical practice, leading to misalignment and at times a lack of mutual understanding and respect.

To overcome this impasse and allow for rapid innovation in mission-critical settings, Barry focused on an interdisciplinary set of participants in innovation and emphasized to his team members the examples of when they had effectively found ways to "work around" traditional organizational charts and the traditional power networks, in the service of an urgent goal.[5] He sought to replicate this rewiring of social networks by putting a couple of very senior and respected physicians on a task force to reshape the rules and structures that defined the innovation pipeline.

Likewise, he sought to bring trusted administrators, with whom he had built decades of experience and respect, into the innovation selection processes—for internal and, importantly, external ecosystem ideas. He explicitly welcomed their input into the experimentation/evaluation cycles that he started to pursue.

We have seen similar approaches work across the military and civilian personnel in defense innovation, including those led by Col. Mike at DIU in Boston, who found that team members from both backgrounds were willing to lean in and help students who came in during the semester to work on scoping out possible areas of focus and mapping the start-up landscape.

Informal political networks cannot simply be wished (or designed) away, and in fact they are not solely a source of conflict or obstruction. Claims over resources, or protectiveness toward contacts and customers, may cause strategic mandates to be ignored or impeded. However, political affiliations can be especially effective in rapidly moving projects forward or gaining access to otherwise complex resources. Meanwhile, overlapping networks can help to link new innovation units and their managers to internal customers and other experts within the organization—ones whom they might know through other shared experiences.

As you choose "who" from your organization should engage the ecosystem stakeholders to drive your innovation priorities, considerations like internal status, membership of key internal networks that matter internally or externally, and organizational politics should be considered alongside more traditional skill sets. Also consider who might lose power in any organizational change and find ways to give them a new role in the change.

Networks based on affiliations such as profession, gender, or age can be especially salient to navigating politics if someone from a group who is otherwise recalcitrant can be co-opted into a leading innovation role. These considerations should therefore be added to your set of criteria as you select the best middle and frontline leaders for your innovation agenda, much as Barry did in building his more inclusive and distributed innovation team.

You may find some people in your organization are intrinsically more political than their colleagues, overly focused on the competitive elements of the organization, like personal self-advancement. It may be worth finding a way to partner with them—as with folk heroes or organizational curmudgeons—to blunt their potential to be obstructive. Even if they are not supportive until they see that political winds are blowing in favor of innovation, they may eventually rally to your innovation effort.

Looking Through the "Cultural" Lens

Culture is not a static, timeless monolith. It evolves, when necessary, especially when its new elements are rewarded and recognized. You will want to resist judging whether your organization's cultural practices and beliefs are right or wrong. Rather, if you understand the reasons for why they exist, and how aspects of them will either help or hinder your efforts to manage change, you will be well positioned to shape a new innovation-oriented culture. This culture will need to build on positive elements of past culture and introduce new and productive elements for the future.

But before you can lead such an effort, you will need to determine the unique elements that characterize your organization (especially those most closely associated with innovation). The challenge you will likely face in analyzing your organization's culture is that it can be hard for insiders to articulate what it is or what it means. As noted in the classic metaphor (which has been attributed to Albert Einstein among others), what does the fish know about the water in which it swims all its life? It is hard for us to understand our own environment because we take it so much for granted. It takes an act of leadership to undertake an honest and open assessment of your organization's specific culture. That said, your frontline workers and middle managers—especially those who are new to your organization or have come from very different workplaces (including from outside organizations)—will have a lot to say and observe: they have only been in the water a short time and so feel its presence more keenly!

At its most simple, culture can be seen through the stories, symbols, and rituals (or routines) of your organization.[6] As you examine these elements, it is worth noting that when it comes to implementing your innovation ecosystem engagement approach (and your wider innovation priorities), nothing in your organization's culture is neutral: it either tends to help such innovation efforts or hinders them.

Start with stories—these are the vignettes we tell people who join, often about the heroes in our organization. In many large organizations that we have worked with, especially those that have been successful for long periods, we have encountered stories of longtime employees who are heroic internal innovators. Or we find stories of those who ideate in their small amount of independent creative time—the famed 20 percent at 3M or a day a week at Google. If this has worked for an important innovation in your organization, it is bound to take on a mythical status. On the one hand, this can inspire others to work hard and use their time wisely. On the other hand, it potentially blocks other approaches to creativity and ideation, such as hackathons, or signals that innovation only comes from the trusted senior researchers alone, not the new hires or external mavericks.

Second come symbols—these can be objects, words, forms of dress, and so on, each of which comes to have a shared meaning for people in your organization. While we often associate symbols with nations (from flags and customary expressions to national costume and sports teams), they are also found in all of our organizations. In academia, they are often the laden bookshelves. In hospitals, as we have mentioned, they are the white coats. In corporations, they may be less obvious but might be the cars that people drive, what people wear on a Friday, who has their own specially prepared meal in a corporate dining room, and so forth. For innovation, it is more likely to be the awards for excellence. If all these are given just for 10-percent-scale innovation projects, and if they are for innovations entirely within well-established areas of technology within the organization, then they send a strong message of what is truly valued. No amount of senior management discussion or prioritization of new innovations at the 10x horizon will be seen as authentic by middle managers if prizes continue to flow only to those in the 10 percent parts of the portfolio. One way to get some insight into an organization's symbols and their meaning is to look at what the lobby of the headquarters looks like—does it showcase innovative ideas, book covers, or expensive artwork?

Last come routines, which, much like stories and symbols, build up around repeated patterns of behavior and beliefs about what works—even if the evidence of effectiveness is no longer clear. Take, for example, the large organizations that have been successful while also being very secretive. Their routines will continue to reinforce secrecy even if it is no longer the most effective way to innovate: it will be taken for granted. When Lockheed's famed skunkworks project to build a jet fighter during World War II is remembered, the habit of secrecy is often seen as the decisive factor in its success. And thus, for a time well beyond the needs of wartime, secrecy became a cultural norm and expectation for innovation.

Not only does this make external ecosystem engagement very hard, but it also probably missed the point: Lockheed's skunkworks were guided by "Kelly Johnson's 14 Rules" that mainly emphasized the routines and rituals of small teams, quick decision-making, and experimentation.[7] Other routines that can help or hinder innovation include the ways in which meetings to evaluate projects are conducted: routines that include learning and challenge, for example by asking the newest person in the room, will drive a different culture than one in which only the most senior team members lead the discussion.

As you determine what is helping and what is hindering your innovation system and therefore your external ecosystem engagement, you will be able to work toward cultural change that supports your rational strategic changes (in line with your well-harnessed political realities).

Leaders like Barry at HHC, Belinda in her government agency, or Mike at MassMutual all know that organizations are organic institutions, full of human beings and their rhythms: they have come into existence, persisted, and evolved, as necessary. As such, the culture of an organization can continue to evolve, and you get to shape the evolution of that organizational culture. Senior leaders, like those we have met throughout this book, get to decide which aspects of the organization's culture they choose to highlight going forward and which ones to downplay. Each choice made by a member of your senior leadership team, along with your middle managers and frontline staff, either reinforces aspects of the existing culture or subtly nudges its evolution in new directions.

If your goal is to drive your innovation priorities though internal and external innovation, especially further out at the innovation horizon, then the direction of change needs to be favorable for innovation. You and your team will want to focus on establishing new habits or new stories, changing the meaning of symbols (or finding new ones), and evolving tried and tested traditions and rituals. Given the subtleties of this task, building (or shifting) an innovation culture is often the hardest and most overlooked aspect of any innovation initiative, and the one for which leadership is the most essential.

Our experience has shown that if you want to improve the chances that your efforts to drive innovation priorities internally—and especially through ecosystem engagement—will be successful, you should consider adapting the stories, symbols, and rituals that have shaped your innovation culture in the past. Reconfigure them, in collaboration with your middle managers and your frontline teams, to amplify the direction of your future efforts. Ensure that they support novelty, expertise (and its associated resources), and experimentation: the three things we know the ecosystem can support and which are often in limited supply in large organizations.

Here are three things to consider to support your ecosystem engagement as it moves out toward the innovation horizons:

- Change the 'stories' that are told, and find new ones that reinforce the ways in which new people—inside and outside—have developed novel solutions across the problem/solution matrix.

- Build new 'symbols' that are more outward-facing by, for example, giving prizes and trophies that recognize ecosystem engagement or external partnerships.
- Design 'rituals and routines' (especially in the evaluation of novel ideas and experiments) that showcase opportunities for learning, rather than just revealing the smartest person in the room or having the "highest paid person's opinion" (HiPPO) be considered correct.

Whatever changes are needed, senior leaders have a big responsibility to live their lives showcasing the new cultural imperatives. If innovation is key but the leader's calendar showcases almost all the time spent on traditional products and projects, then the innovation message may be rejected.

Returning to our friend Dr. Barry, introducing innovation at the HHC system was not only a nicety but also a way to improve life and death outcomes. But his own cultural work was as important as the strategic planning he had painstakingly accomplished. He knew he had to start telling more stories to highlight the innovations that were not just of heroic surgeons on their feet for twenty-four hours or inventing new approaches in moments of crisis. His team started to tell stories of young PhD students in AI who worked with emergency department nurses at HHC to develop a nurse scheduling algorithm to optimize nurse supply and patient demand. Their collaboration resulted in the whole department being more streamlined and efficient—an innovation in the SN zone (a reasonably novel solution to a problem that had frustrated the hospital teams for years).

Barry also needed to change the rituals of the hospital. He expanded from the somewhat intimidating hospital rounds, where leading physicians asked hard questions to young trainees, to daily stand-up workgroup meetings where teams of nurses, technicians, and physicians all worked on 10 percent innovations in rapid experimentation cycles.

And last were the symbols, so richly textured in a hospital setting steeped in tradition. What would help? In Barry's organization, it was about celebrating people talking about failure so others could learn from it (both in the immediate aftermath and over a longer time frame)—a cultural behavior essential in building a highly reliable organization. In this practice, Barry was aligned with another former student of ours who was leading an innovation program in his academic dental hospital—a "failure prize." Barry's colleague had borrowed a ritual from the military—the "hotwash," which is a debrief that happens right after emergency situations—to see what went wrong and identify areas for improvement (with the name originating from the "hot water" one would use to clean their kit right after a mission). Uniquely, what the team had added was a new symbol—a prize awarded for the most powerful lesson from failure. This is perhaps not the answer for us all, but it is something to ponder as we explore how to shift the cultural fabric of our organizations to deliver on our innovation priorities.

Understand and Address Culture Clashes in the Ecosystem

Just as the "three lenses" are a useful framework for examining one's own organization, they can also prove useful for understanding the other stakeholders in the innovation ecosystem and their interactions with you and each other.

You don't need to do a deep dive into the internal politics and cultures of all your ecosystem partners. But bear in mind that all organizations—being full of people—harbor as many complexities as your own. Recall that when choosing frontline entrepreneurial leaders, you are looking for people who can appreciate and participate in the culture of a given type of stakeholder. The same person is unlikely to be on the same wavelengths as all of the entrepreneurs, university professors, and partners in a VC firm. You might even use the "three lenses" to choose entrepreneurial leaders who have the "right" social network affiliations and cultural sensibilities in your organization but who can also network out into the ecosystem and blend into the culture of ecosystem stakeholders, so that they can effectively engage both the internal and the external cultures.

It is not easy to select individuals with the ability to connect to the different cultures of the ecosystem and who can also work within your large organization. You are asking people to be "cosmopolitan"—appreciating and fitting in with more than one culture—and that is often a challenge. Culture clash among stakeholders is common (as we see in our efforts with multistakeholder teams!), and so is the clash that your ecosystem-facing leaders will face as they work out in the ecosystem and then come back in and deal with your own internal system. It is worth understanding these various tensions because they can ultimately drive many of the frustrations and failures that cause even the most strategic of engagement efforts to falter.

Innovation leaders should understand the reasons for the differences among these cultures and find ways to manage them. In our experience, culture clashes come in various flavors but most frequently manifest as tension around the time frames by which each of the different types of organizations operate. And in turn, these time frames are shaped by different definitions of the incentives and priorities of the stakeholders. We explore these two elements in turn.

When it comes to time, entrepreneurs universally feel that large organizations are slow (and they may have chosen entrepreneurship as a career because they prefer the pace and flexibility of a start-up). VCs are often quite fast—not least because they work on an investment time frame that is closely aligned to entrepreneurial experimentation cycles. Their cadence is so widely shared from one VC to another that the vast majority schedule their meetings to make investment choices on an industry-standard Monday morning! All three apex stakeholders—university spinouts, other entrepreneurs, and risk capital providers—condemn governments as bureaucratic when we ask them to caricature one another. And all are certain that the academic and administrative parts of universities are unnecessarily slow and fail to see the "real-world" urgency of the challenges around them.

While some of these character sketches are overblown, they are often grounded in the realities of actual cultures and in deliberate strategic choices, determined by the incentives of the people working in particular settings. When the incentives change, the culture can too. With innovation ecosystem engagement, recognizing the incentives and mission of the different stakeholders can go some way toward reducing culture clash. And cultural mismatches can be overcome, at least in part by an appreciation for the others' approach to time, and alignment, through more explicit conversations.

To understand large organizations (public or private), it is important to recognize that they optimize for careful, long-term operational excellence, whether they are selling products and services for profit or executing a public mission. Many of their internal objectives, system designs, and metrics are aligned for those purposes. They typically focus on near-term competitiveness, through delivery of BAU, monthly check-ins, quarterly earnings, annual budgets, and yearly or more frequent employee appraisal cycles that keep the business on track. Some parts of the large organization—such as strategy or R&D units—may have longer delivery cycles, but they too have to follow the rhythm of their wider business and of those who fund them, whether market investors or ministries of finance. Therefore, most employees respond to their leaders' priorities, and the structure of their budget cycles, by producing results in those monthly, quarterly, and annual cycles. And they are compensated with salaries and bonuses accordingly.

Entrepreneurs, like Bob Mumgaard, Natalya Bailey, Lorenz Meier, and others whom we have met in this book, work differently. Instead of incrementally improving existing products and services for current customers, they are pursuing sophisticated technological solutions with a goal to ultimately build the first-of-a-kind product or system to show their customers the value that they can generate. Before validating and building this large-scale, expensive system, they will be cycling through experiments that reduce risks in a systematic way, taking the time they need while also being as frugal with cash as their plan allows. Rather than the daily share price, they may be focused on their monthly rate of cash burn, with an eye on a potentially enormous impact and (perhaps) payout when their start-up is acquired or goes public in five to ten years.

Other stakeholders in the innovation ecosystem are likely to have different objectives and metrics, with different time frames for showing results. In the university setting, for instance, from MIT to Dalhousie to ETH Zurich, the various players will be planning their work around the academic semesters or their multiyear research projects. Graduate students have a sense of focus and urgency around the time horizons of completing their master's (one to two years) or PhD thesis (four to five years) and finding jobs. And junior faculty, especially those early on the tenure track, will be looking to publish at pace and maintain their intellectual edge at the innovation horizon over other competing labs and teams worldwide.

At a university, the dominant culture, however, may be that of the tenured faculty who are focused on securing grants, among other funding, to run their SME-like laboratories with their students and postdocs. If the university has a publish-or-perish policy for granting tenure, then junior tenure-track faculty, graduate students, and postdocs who want academic careers will focus on producing papers from their research, rather than creating patents or products that can be commercialized. On the other hand, if the university chooses to reward patenting and spinouts, then the university culture will be more oriented toward generating licensable IP and impact at scale, and the university is more likely working with other ecosystem members.

Risk capital providers may look for returns over different time periods, depending on the nature of their investment (digital or deep tech) and its innovation stage. They have a higher risk appetite than commercial banks, insurers, and asset managers; that is, they are comfortable with a lower success rate in exchange for potentially greater reward. This is especially true of the frontline GPs who decide which entrepreneurs to back, and are themselves more entrepreneurial than the LPs who allocate capital to them.

Innovation through ecosystem engagement is a long-term endeavor, and long-term relationships with a diverse set of external stakeholders count. Many leaders have deep relationships with mentors and bosses, colleagues, and competitors. But it can be challenging to foster such relationships outside of an organization or career path. Innovation leaders in large organizations must commit to the ecosystem even as they and their colleagues focus on the short-run concerns of BAU and opportunities for greater levels of promotion and leadership. They must do so while the stakeholders themselves are also dealing with their own immediate goals and often their longer-term desires for ecosystem interactions. These shared goals are the source of much of the goodwill that we have encountered in our ecosystem engagement work and are an important foundation for learning and cooperation among stakeholders.

Learn from Other Ecosystem Mindsets

Given that cultures are not static, some of the external stakeholders' cultures may productively rub off on your large organization. One of the best ways innovation leaders can change their internal "system" and its culture is to expose some of its members to the way other stakeholders work. This is especially what leaders often mean when they talk about bringing in a more "entrepreneurial mindset." Of course, this presupposes that cultures can be separated from priorities and incentives, which, as we have illustrated above, is unlikely to be the case. But if your organization really wants to reshape its priorities around the wider innovation horizon, then both strategic and cultural change are important, and cultural elements are worth learning and absorbing from the ecosystem along with the novelty, resources, and experimentation we have described.

For example, large organization middle managers and frontline staff might learn from entrepreneurs how to work quickly through ideas and find ways to replicate some of these processes. Or they may encounter new ways of looking at technology trends by engaging with entrepreneurs, university faculty, or risk capital providers. As important as these strategic activities (which can be learned and brought into the innovation pipeline) are the associated cultural elements. Watching who speaks up and how during a pitch meeting between a VC and an entrepreneur can be as instructive as the questions asked: it is a window into learning and experimentation. Listening to the questions in a PhD seminar and seeing how and why a research project is deemed important can illustrate how the furthest horizon is being constructed—something that is often hard to experience inside a corporate or government office.

Innovation leaders can facilitate encounters that prompt new internal practices by using the three lenses framework to identify areas in the organization that might be politically willing or culturally open to them. You could place a middle manager or a frontline entrepreneurial staff member with a particular skill set as a mentor to an accelerator program, where they would learn fresh ways of thinking or how to seize on unexpected ideas. Your leaders could be encouraged to invite entrepreneurs to visit internal teams to discuss how they work. Senior leaders could get a fresh perspective on emerging technology trends by meeting with the GPs of VC funds.

Barry gained support for his innovation initiative at HHC by giving some of his leaders the opportunity to meet and learn from stakeholders whom they might not naturally encounter: not just to learn from but also to become part of a very different world.

We have brought government leaders from around the globe to MIT and have often been hosted by our friend and colleague Vlad (whom we met earlier in the book) so that they could learn about the emerging future of nanomaterials and the role of specialized infrastructure like MIT.nano in supporting the novel ideas being generated by faculty, students, entrepreneurs, and some corporations. The playful "10^{-9}" T-shirts and pins (bearing the mathematical representation of the nanoscale) are as much a part of the visit as the serious technical discussions. The thousands of names etched on a giant silicon wafer are another! They are a reminder that generating novelty requires effort, energy, and a willingness to play with ideas (a perspective beautifully captured in E. O. Wilson's book *Letters to a Young Scientist*).[8]

Barry was astute in connecting the right people. Without his efforts, senior leaders at the hospital might not have otherwise met with risk capital providers. But in doing so, they learned about different ways to deploy their capital budgets to support small-scale innovations that could be expanded in subsequent innovation cycles: an insight that helped Barry and his team gather the resources they needed to work with the ecosystem to access additional unique and specialized resources. Mike Fanning at MassMutual similarly moved an entire team to Boston to ensure that his people were connected with the exciting work happening downstairs at MC. This was done not just for the demo day when all the pitches were pitch-perfect but also during the run-up, when teams were stress-tested, experiments were not working, and plans had to be redefined. This helped the large organization's staff recognize that novel ideas don't start out as clearly articulated as they thought. It also lowered the barriers to their own people making new suggestions and helped foster a stronger understanding of structured experimentation.

The culture of place-based innovation ecosystems as a whole, meanwhile, is shifting. Getting the right people together is increasingly difficult, not to mention allowing for serendipitous encounters. Even in an ecosystem defined by geography, hybrid work is making it harder to schedule formal meetings, much less meet up in a coffee shop or for after-work drinks. Establishing in-office (or in-lab) expectations such as all-at-work Wednesdays can help coordinate innovation teams internally. Externally, we wait to see whether "first Monday of the month," "tech Tuesdays," or "Friday drinks" meetups continue, or if new opportunities for chance encounters between stakeholders evolve. There is likely to be a competitive advantage for those ecosystems, and their stakeholders, who find a way to be together for the early, more creative cycles of innovation. In-person time is likely to be a precious commodity for your organization, one that strongly shapes cultural exchange and is essential to really tap into the novelty, resources, and experimental culture that ecosystems have to offer.

Create a Context That Supports Innovation

This chapter takes the insights from chapter 5 using a "strategic design" perspective and strengthens your approach to innovation through the two other lenses: political and cultural. There may be new insights for you as a senior leader, or for your enabling middle managers and frontline teams, from both lenses that strengthen the design of the internal system and support your external ecosystem engagement. In some ways, as senior leaders architecting the system, you are making the most readily visible signs of commitment about your organizational commitment to innovation. But the alignment of the political and cultural elements will also strengthen your efforts and drive the sorts of outcomes you need.

The three lenses, taken together, give leaders a rounded perspective on the capacity of their organization to support innovation, especially out at the further horizon where risk is high but the need to operate is strong. Leaders can more effectively navigate the external innovation landscape when they identify the people and places in their organization that are most likely to embrace innovation—or at least reserve judgment—enlisting their support. But of the three, culture is the hardest to see through and change. Having a clearer picture of it can determine whether the innovation priorities you wish to emphasize are likely to be seen as audacious but possible or as another piece of innovation theater.

No organizations can predict the future, so they can't know exactly how innovation will serve them. Engaging with other leaders of large organizations in your local ecosystem can help share good practice and lessons learned: a great Boston-based example is the "innovation leader" network that brings together corporate professionals.[9] Having an internal system that supports innovation—with people who will advocate for it and a culture that can absorb it—makes organizations stronger. Pursuing innovation priorities with a strong system, within a set of ecosystem relationships, makes organizations resilient.

Key Points from Chapter 6: Political and Cultural Challenges

Having identified the different levels of leaders in an organization, and which roles each should play, it is important to address other organizational challenges to innovation:

- The *three lenses* approach to organizations encourages a focus on issues beyond the rational "strategic design," such as the political and cultural dimensions.
- Applied specifically to efforts at innovation, the "three lenses" highlight the political and cultural challenges that leaders are likely to encounter:

- ○ The political lens has leaders view their organization to identify where supporters and obstacles are likely to be (irrespective of the org chart). Politically savvy leaders will know how to get things done.

- ○ The cultural dimension is important but harder to describe, as each organization has its own culture, revealed through stories, symbols. and routines. Culturally aware leaders know where the friction is likely to be.

- When engaging others, there can be a "culture clash" with the different stakeholders, so it is worth considering who to send out into the external ecosystem to achieve your goals.

- It is also possible to learn from other ecosystem mindsets, such as that of the entrepreneur.

Turning to chapter 7, we will look at how large organizations can both "do good" in their own terms and "do well" for the ecosystems they engage.

7 "Doing Good" While Also "Doing Well"

This book focuses on how you can lead your organization to "do well" at innovation by engaging ecosystems for near- and medium-term competitive benefit and by helping shape ecosystems to serve as a source of strategic advantage in the long term. Of course, the reality of life in large organizations is that if there are no quick wins from innovation for the business or the mission, then neither the individuals nor the enterprise will find it easy to stick with it. Leaders may give up on ecosystem engagement or revert to innovation theater—public displays, like a one-time hackathon or a gleaming new office, that are ultimately fruitless without commitment behind them. As a senior leader in the organization, you may struggle to maintain commitment given that the time horizon for meaningful outputs from innovation might make it challenging to match the pace of expectations.

Our advice is to build a long-term plan that prioritizes what you really must accomplish for the future success of your organization: the "what" that articulates a clear vision of the horizon. You should then focus on optimizing your chances to be effective and do well at innovation in reasonable time frames that match those of your organization, that is, by managing the "who" and the "how." In the near term, we recognize—from our research in many large organizations—that you must show tangible results in less than year, often talking instead about months. In the "medium term," we know that many large organizations use a one- to three-year time frame: this often tracks the job (or posting) duration of many of the middle and frontline leaders you are working with as well as the resource allocation commitments. Thus, it is important to be realistic about the time frames involved. Given that much "culture clash" among stakeholders in an innovation ecosystem comes from differing time frames, you as a leader will want to match your internal system's needs with what we know about the time frames in the ecosystem, which we have represented with innovation "cycles."

That said, we have also found that it is essential to additionally consider the long-term opportunities that come from committing to sustained ecosystem engagement. Building relationships today will yield insight and inputs into key priorities, but they will also lay the foundations of long-term novelty, specialized resources, and an experimental culture. We have argued that there is a strategic benefit for large organizations to take a longer view of their external relationships in some specific locations that hold the most promise of future benefits.

Ecosystem engagement offers large organizations a way to prepare for the future. But as a leader, you will need clear priorities. And you will need to go after them with the right people and processes while allowing space for those people to see over the horizon and into those whitespaces—to discover what they have not imagined—and to benefit from the serendipity that characterizes some of the more creative places on the planet.

Beyond specific projects or interactions, being a part of the social fabric of key innovation ecosystems will, in the long run, be of significant value to your organization. As such, it is important for you to truly understand the perspective of your peers among the key ecosystem stakeholders—"what" they need, "who" matters to when, and "how" do they want to engage—so that you build reciprocal and trusted relationships over time. These will be valuable for your organization, your teams, and to each person individually in their careers.

As a leader with a clear set of priorities, tapping into structured innovation processes happening in the wild of the ecosystem offers you a way to overcome the short-termism that leads to so many innovation failures. Cycles of experimentation and learning, through which researchers and entrepreneurs test their ideas and their business models, are designed to deliver a series of short-term results on a path toward medium- and long-term impact. Over a slightly longer time frame than may be expected for an incremental improvement to BAU, large organizations can still do well against their familiar success criteria.

"Doing Well" Can Lead to "Doing Good"

By doing well in place-based ecosystems, large organizations might also "do good" for these places in the medium term and possibly the wider communities in which they are nested.

Large organizations do not suddenly need to become selflessly altruistic to do good. They can, however, easily identify how it may be in their enlightened self-interest (for medium- and long-term advantage) to invest more in the development of their local ecosystems in ways that drive mutual benefit and build trust.

Government agencies might increase the number of start-ups solving a mission through taking a more reliable acquisition role as major customers. They could have new solutions deployed while also boosting regional economic development and tax revenue. (This is in addition to those government development agencies that have, as their primary objective, the economic development of a region, but these too may wish to consider the innovation ecosystem approach to regions' comparative advantage, rather than relying on public subsidies or attracting foreign direct investment.)

For-profit companies may be less inclined to consider the spillover benefits, yet with careful attention to their objectives, their ecosystem engagement may just provide them. As the entirely global distribution of supply chains and sourcing of talent lose their charm in a more geopolitical world, a firm might wish to encourage more regional suppliers or deepen the bench of local service providers, such as lawyers and investors, in the ecosystems that it chooses to engage. As a result, the individual innovation ecosystems become stronger, with more resources shared among all the stakeholders: other corporations, start-up ventures, the local universities, and even the government.

A Virtuous Circle

Doing well in place-based ecosystems may even create a virtuous circle of interaction and engagement that benefits all parties and ensures that the outcomes for the whole of society are greater than the sum of their efforts.

Economic prosperity can be a side benefit when organizations pursue ecosystem growth locally. Enrico Moretti has outlined how high-skilled jobs in innovation ecosystems (while small in number) might have outsized knock-on, multiplier benefits.[1] In his study of the US job market, he posited that there was a "5x" employment multiplier from jobs in digital IDEs; they created the indirect demand for five other jobs in the places that they were located. For companies in deep-tech IDEs, that multiplier is likely even higher and comes with job creation along the entire spectrum from science to engineering to construction. (Deep-tech IDEs are also even less likely to relocate than digital-tech ones that are much more mobile, thus providing a key deep-tech anchor point in the innovation ecosystem.) Such job growth might be seen as a social good in its own right or as contributing to the growth of a local customer base with greater purchasing power. Either way, the local community is likely to welcome the increase in employment opportunities.

For example, the cybersecurity mission of the National Cyber Force (NCF) in the United Kingdom has considerable importance to the government: it also anchors, and is supported by, the development of a "cyber corridor" from Manchester north to the Lake District.[2] This emerging ecosystem has brought together the University of Manchester and the University of Lancaster, with large corporations including the defense company BAE Systems and the regional government. It meets the needs of the government's NCF while providing better training, and more jobs, locally. Additionally, it fosters a growing set of specialized resources and experimentation opportunities that attract more people and novel ideas, which in turn benefits BAE Systems and also, over time, the universities.

Large organizations may even help regional ecosystems evolve in ways that meet long-term society-wide goals. To see why this is the case, we only have to look at the trends that are likely to shape innovation in the decades ahead: the evolving nature of our relationship to place, the spread of innovation ecosystems to new countries and continents, and the geopolitical fault lines that influence whether and how much to engage with particular countries. Each of these trends will inform our decisions of where to seek novelty of ideas, resources, and opportunities for experimentation.

Location Matters

Place-based ecosystems will continue to be a significant source of innovation in the foreseeable future. This is in large part because the reasons that spur their creation and growth will largely continue to hold true. Despite many new digital communication technologies, crises in financial capitalism, and the acceleration of virtual work environments, geography—and most importantly the proximity of individuals to one another as they challenge the status quo and develop new ideas—still matter for innovation, especially in the earliest stages, and in the deeper technologies.

Regional leaders who are charged with nurturing ecosystems in rural or distributed locations are working hard to overcome the challenges of distance. Yet, the pull of colocation in urban areas, especially in the early stages of innovation when novelty is at its highest and uncertainty needs specialized resources and experimentation, remains strong.

Ecosystems Are Developing Globally

In fact, the number of urban innovation ecosystems is growing. Leaders in regions around the world are learning from mature ecosystems in places like Greater Boston, Silicon Valley, Singapore, and London about how to accelerate innovation in the places that matter to them.

This means that if your organization operates primarily in one area of the world, there may be ecosystems emerging where you are. And for those that are more geographically agnostic, there are new sources of novelty and richness to explore and partners to engage around the world—from Lima to Lagos, Rio to Riyadh, Munich to Malaysia, Cairo to Cape Town, and Tokyo to Thailand.

Meanwhile, individuals are more mobile and can choose to move to places that matter to them. After working in a mature ecosystem, they could bring their experiences and expertise home, where a developing ecosystem may benefit considerably. Add to this centripetal force the fact that digital technology allows for efficiencies in accessing some specialized resources remotely, and ecosystems can survive at a smaller scale.

Geopolitical Considerations Are Intensifying

Innovation ecosystems are multiplying just as the global economy is reorganizing. Our world is becoming multipolar (again) and more competitive. The previous forty years of increasingly open global connectivity, with hyperefficient supply chains crisscrossing the planet (with little regard to externalities), is giving way to coalitions of like-minded nations and the development of regional networks that share priorities and ultimately share some of the fruits of their collective innovation efforts.

Leaders will have to consider more than maximizing profits when they make decisions about their global operations—including the placement of factories, supply chain routes, and locations of data storage. They will come to prioritize resilience to supply chain shocks and geopolitical competition, as well as compliance with regional norms or home-country rules for environment sustainability, social responsibility, and data privacy.[3]

When organizations choose innovation partners, it will matter which country the start-up and its founders come from and where they have sourced their risk capital. They will have to take a geopolitical perspective when they decide where to engage, focusing on trusted ecosystems, especially for technological solutions that are of strategic relevance to economic or national security.

A Shared Identity and Mission

For-profit businesses are under more pressure from governments, and society at large, to consider the needs of all their stakeholders when making decisions. It's no longer sufficient for most companies to fulfill their environment, social, and governance (ESG) obligations through regulatory compliance, philanthropy, and employee volunteering.

Meanwhile, governments around the world are committing to the United Nations (UN) Sustainable Development Goals, which aim to end poverty, hunger, AIDS, and discrimination against women and girls, as well as support the UN Convention on Climate Change. These public agreements promote public goods that might not otherwise arise if left to self-interested parties—whether private companies or public agencies.

Ecosystems provide a platform for sharing goals with a broader public mission, facilitating the integration of global initiatives and local actions.

Our MIT offices in Kendall Square overlook construction projects that seem not to have ceased work since the late 2010s (save for a few quiet months at the start of the pandemic). Here, we can see the fruits of the virtuous cycle in the place-based innovation ecosystem. Commitments by MIT to invest in the local area, including redeveloping tracts of unused land, regenerating old industrial spaces, and building new academic departments, are a way to "do well" for the Institute—for its endowment, its students, staff, and faculty—while also "doing good" for the local ecosystem and the diverse communities in which it is nested.

Over time, and in partnership with the local government and other stakeholders, MIT has systematically developed more plans for local housing and living. Property values have increased and, with them, the returns to the institution. But the investments in the community—and the innovation that has been spurred by the chance interactions among professors, entrepreneurs, investors, and corporate leaders—have led to extraordinary benefits. Doing well has led, with some careful shaping and listening, to doing good. The ongoing challenge will be to make sure the innovation ecosystem benefits the local communities in even more tangible ways.

Finally, as is the case for Kendall Square (the self-styled "most innovative square mile on the planet"), for the UK Cyber Corridor, or Israel's Startup Nation, the stakeholders in the ecosystem develop a shared sense of identity and become part of the social fabric that we have described as being so important to innovation ecosystems. This shared identity can help large organizations gain a broader license to operate, while these mutually reinforcing activities create a virtuous cycle driven by a now shared mission.

Intersection of Our Innovation Ecosystem and Corporate Innovation Work

This book sits at the intersection between two major themes in our joint work—namely innovation ecosystems (where ecosystem builders seek to achieve comparative advantage through innovation) and corporate innovation (where we started helping for-profit businesses seek competitive advantage through innovation but soon discovered it also attracted government and nonprofits).

Our innovation ecosystem focus (https://innovationecosystems.mit.edu) emphasizes advising leaders in multistakeholder regions around the world, especially with our MIT colleagues through the global MIT REAP program (https://reap.mit.edu) and its global alumni network, as well as in classes. We focus there on how leaders might realistically assess their region's capacities for innovation and entrepreneurship so they can identify areas of comparative advantage and intervene strategically to accelerate "innovation-driven entrepreneurship."[4] The leaders are often trying to do good for a region, whether their own or an overseas one.

Our corporate innovation focus (https://corporateinnovation.mit.edu) is on advising leaders, in the public and private sectors, through MIT Sloan's Executive Education and Executive MBA (EMBA) programs where we teach, and also more directly.[5] We focus on how these leaders might best achieve successful, strategic, and sustainable advantage from innovation and the practices of entrepreneurship (https://exec.mit.edu/s/topic/corporate -innovation).[6] In this setting, we emphasize that leaders should, of course, help their organizations do well but that there may be strategic benefit by strengthening the ecosystems that matter (i.e., also doing good).

In writing this book, we have illustrated that a closer link between doing well and doing good in the world is possible through innovation-driven entrepreneurship. In fact, the interests of large organizations seeking to innovate through ecosystem engagement can align with those seeking to strengthen the innovation ecosystem through multistakeholder engagement.

There are, of course, challenges with the different time frames, vocabularies, and metrics that govern each stakeholder's business. Yet, it is in the interests of all parties to find ways to collaborate. To that end, we will continue to uncover the connections between these strands—for the mutual benefit of all communities and their leaders.

In turn, we hope you will find these frameworks useful and that you too might contribute, as prior executives and leaders have done, to helping us evolve our thinking. To that end, we look forward to hearing from others who are also on this journey.

Acknowledgments

On innovation ecosystems, we are grateful to our colleagues and to the hundreds of ecosystem stakeholders with whom we have worked over that decade (e.g., in MIT's global REAP, Regional Entrepreneurship Acceleration Program).[1] This has allowed us to test our hypotheses, such as the world having remained "spiky" (rather than become flat) when it comes to innovation, with teams from all the inhabited continents. While each region faces specific challenges, the global trend of forces concentrating innovation unevenly is constantly emerging.

On innovation in large organizations, we are also grateful to the hundreds of leaders of large organizations, from those taking our corporate innovation courses in Executive Education and our seminars through MIT Corporate Relations, to those in our classes, for example, in MIT Sloan's Executive MBA (EMBA) program, or participating in our direct (confidential) consultancy. This has confirmed the trend of large organizations struggling to adapt to technological change and adopt innovation in strategically beneficial ways. Common challenges include the structure (and culture) of such organizations being optimized for "business as usual," whereas the trend and pace of technology and innovation require a nimbler approach.

Appendix: Getting Started

Taking all these insights and frameworks into innovation, ecosystems, and their many stakeholders, we wished to conclude with a short section on getting started. Given our definition of innovation, it is important that it aim to result in some "impact." With all these challenges, it is therefore worth sharing what we have learned from our research, and from leaders who have taken forward such innovation efforts:

- Nothing succeeds like success, so it is worth planning on a "quick win" or two.
- Set a near-term period—such as "ninety days"—in which you will show progress.
- This is initially likely to be a "little i" innovation (rather than a "Big I" one).
- Our new "Accelerating Innovation" sprint might be a way to formulate this.[1]
- Secure "air cover" from your immediate boss(es), with negotiated guardrails.
- It is easier to achieve a quick win in the part of the system the boss oversees.
- Have more than one option in case your first choice does not work out in time.
- Identify a "coalition of the willing" likely to help you achieve your goal.
- Secure the resources—including time and space away from BAU—to do this.
- After this ninety-day innovation cycle, know what options you will suggest next.
- Plant the seeds during the ninety days so that your next options are ready to go.

Notes

Introduction

1. The "varieties of capitalism" literature—influenced by *Varieties of Capitalism: The Institutional Foundations of Comparative Advantage* by Peter A. Hall and David Soskie (Oxford: Oxford University Press, 2001)—swiftly turned to innovation as one of the key outputs of different national varieties (especially the US "liberal market" versus the German "coordinated market" models of capitalism).

2. Deborah Ancona, Elaine Backman, and Kate Isaacs, "Nimble Leadership: Walking the Line between Creativity and Chaos," *Harvard Business Review* (July–August 2019): 74–83, https://hbr.org/2019/07/nimble-leadership.

Chapter 1

1. Joel Mokyr, *The Enlightened Economy: An Economic History of Britain 1700–1850* (New Haven, CT: Yale University Press, 2009); Joel Mokyr, "Entrepreneurship and the Industrial Revolution in Britain," in *The Invention of Enterprise*, ed. David S. Landes, Joel Mokyr, and William Baumol (Princeton, NJ: Princeton University Press, 2012).

2. Jonathan Rothwell, José Lobo, Deborah Strumsky, and Mark Muro, "Patenting and Innovation in Metropolitan America," Brookings, February 1, 2013, https://www.brookings.edu/articles/patenting-and-innovation-in-metropolitan-america/.

3. Phil Budden, Fiona Murray, and Anna Turskaya, "Assessing the System and Capacities in 'Innovation-Driven Entrepreneurship' Ecosystems" (working paper v3.0, MIT REAP, 2024), https://reap.mit.edu/resource/assessing-the-system-and-capacities.

4. In 2012, the president of MIT at the time (Rafael Reif) tasked his "MIT Innovation Initiative" (MITii) with defining "innovation" as part of its initial commission. This definition remains current, as seen in Tim Miano and Fiona Murray's 2024 retrospective report on universities as "Innovation Systems: Blueprints and Lessons from MIT," https://www.innovation-blueprints.com, and in the work of MIT's Innovation Headquarters (iHQ; https://ihq.mit.edu).

5. Research is ongoing, but early evidence confirms that colocation remains high in both knowledge and manufacturing, with industry clusters being very agglomerated and strongly correlated with knowledge intensity (see Mercedes Delgado, "The Co-Location of Innovation and Production in Clusters," *Industry and Innovation* 27, no. 8 [2020]: 842–870). MIT has produced research to address this question; see David Atkin, Keith Chen, and Anton Popov, "The Returns to Face-to-Face Interactions: Knowledge Spillovers in Silicon Valley" (NBER working paper no. 30147, 2022), https://www.nber.org/papers/w30147. Evidence also suggests that remote work leads to more siloes, fewer unexpected network connections, and less innovation. See Longqi Yang et al., "The Effects of remote work on collaboration among information workers," *Nature* (2022), https://www.nature.com/articles/s41562-021-01196-4.

6. Henry Etzkowitz, *The Triple Helix: University–Industry–Government Innovation and Entrepreneurship*, rev. ed. (New York: Routledge, 2017).

7. Fawry, home page, accessed November 11, 2024, https://www.fawry.com; Vezeeta, home page, accessed November 11, 2024, https://www.vezeeta.com/en.

8. Robert Fairlie and Sameeksha Desai, *National Report on Early-Stage Entrepreneurship in the United States: 2020* (Kansas City, MO: Ewing Marion Kauffman Foundation, 2021).

9. Mercedes Delgado and Fiona E. Murray, "Faculty as Catalysts for Training New Inventors: Differential Outcomes for Male and Female PhD Students," *Proceedings of the National Academy of Sciences* 118, no. 45 (2021), https://doi.org/10.1073/pnas.2200684120.

10. Naomi Hausman, "University Innovation, Local Economic Growth, and Entrepreneurship" (working paper, Social Science Research Network, 2012), https://papers.ssrn.com/sol3/papers.cfm?abstract_id=2097842.

11. DSM, home page, accessed November 11, 2024, https://www.dsm.com/corporate/home.html.

12. Maria Gallucci and Jeff St. John, "6 Innovative Startups That Are Kicking CO_2 Out of Cement and Concrete," Canary Media, October 24, 2023, https://www.canarymedia.com/articles/clean-industry/6-innovative-start-ups-that-are-kicking-co2-out-of-cement-and-concrete.

13. This definition builds on the 1999 McKinsey "three-horizon" approach, out to the distant "horizon three," but that plotted company value over time to assist businesspeople with strategic capital allocation for growth. See "Enduring Ideas: The Three Horizons of Growth," *McKinsey Quarterly*, December 1, 2009, https://www.mckinsey.com/capabilities/strategy-and-corporate-finance/our-insights/enduring-ideas-the-three-horizons-of-growth. Our approach is less deterministic and more relative over the concept of "novelty." A technology may be new to you without being new to the world.

14. For background on the Toyota Way, see Michael Cusumano, *The Japanese Auto-mobile Industry: Technology and Management at Nissan and Toyota* (Cambridge, MA: Harvard University Press, 1986).

15. Eric von Hippel, *Democratizing Innovation* (Cambridge, MA: MIT Press, 2005).

16. MIT.nano Announces Founding Members of Its Corporate Consortium," MIT News, July 8, 2019, https://news.mit.edu/2019/mit-nano-announces-corporate-con sortium-founding-members-0708.

17. "Held in High Regard—Nova Scotia Is Home to the Highest Concentration of Ocean Scientists in the World," Pro-Oceanus, November 20, 2012, https://pro -oceanus.com/about/news?c=held-in-high-regard-nova-scotia-is-home-to-the-highest -concentration-of-ocean-scientists-in-the-world.

18. Williams Johns, "The Motorsport Valley: The Biggest Hub of Motor Racing in the World," Medium, July 26, 2019, https://medium.com/inside-the-motorsport -valley-the-biggest-hub-of/the-motorsport-valley-the-biggest-hub-of-motor-racing -in-the-world-ab13e16e4d36.

Chapter 2

1. The full nine-stage TRL process was developed by NASA; see Catherine G. Manning, "Technology Readiness Levels," NASA, September 27, 2023, https://www.nasa .gov/directorates/somd/space-communications-navigation-program/technology -readiness-levels/.

2. Reference to NASA's collaboration with the Perth-based mining sector. See "Taking Mining Technology into Orbit," CSIRO, April 18, 2023, https://www.csiro .au/en/news/All/Articles/2023/April/Taking-mining-technology-into-orbit.

3. "Unknown unknowns" comes from NASA from at least the 1980s, though it was popularized by others in the early twenty-first century. See United States Congress House Committee on Science and Technology. Subcommittee on Space Science and Applications, *NASA Program Management and Procurement Procedures and Practices: Hearings before the Subcommittee on Space Science and Applications of the Committee on Science and Technology, Ninety-Seventh Congress, First Session, June 24, 25, 1981* (Washington, DC: US Government Printing Office, 1981), 73–74, 82, 89, 92, 98, and 115, https://www.google.com/books/edition/NASA_Program_Management_and_Procure ment/W2sVAAAAIAAJ?hl=en&gbpv=0.

4. Paul D. Kretkowski, "The 15 Percent Solution," *Wired*, January 23, 1998, https:// www.wired.com/1998/01/the-15-percent-solution/; "Founders' IPO Letter," Alphabet Investor Relations, accessed November 11, 2024, https://abc.xyz/investor/founders -letters/ipo-letter/.

5. Phil Budden, Fiona Murray, Isaac Rahamin, Dylan Brown, and Nick Setterberg, "Kessel Run: An Innovation Opportunity for the US Air Force" (Mission Innovation working paper, 2021; on Murray Lab website), https://murray-lab.org/wp-content /uploads/2024/08/Kessel-Run_compressed.pdf. The fuller story is now set out by Raj Shah and Christopher Kirchoff in *Unit X: How the Pentagon and Silicon Valley Are Transforming the Future of War* (New York City: Simon & Schuster, 2024).

6. Ling Zhu, *Quantum Computing: Concepts, Current State, and Considerations for Congress* (Washington, DC: Congressional Research Service, 2023).

7. Michael Bogobowicz, Rodney Zemmel, Scarlett Gao, Mateusz Masiowski, Niko Mohr, and Henning Soller, "Quantum Technology Sees Record Investments, Progress on Talent Gap," McKinsey Digital, April 24, 2023, https://www.mckinsey.com /capabilities/mckinsey-digital/our-insights/quantum-technology-sees-record-invest ments-progress-on-talent-gap.

Chapter 3

1. Scott Malone, "GE's Immelt Hopes Move to Boston Fuels Staff 'Paranoia,'" Reuters, March 2016, https://www.reuters.com/article/ge-headquarters/ges-immelt -hopes-move-to-boston-fuels-staff-paranoia-idINL2N16W12L/.

2. Andrew Small, "Why GE Moved to Boston, According to Its CEO," Bloomberg, September 29, 2016, https://www.bloomberg.com/news/articles/2016-09-29/why -general-electric-moved-to-boston.

3. Phil Budden, Fiona Murray, and Ogbogu Ukuku, "Differentiating Small Enterprises in the Innovation Economy: Start-Ups, New SMEs, and Other Growth Ventures" (working paper, REAP, 2021), https://reap.mit.edu/assets/Differentiating-Small -Enterprises-IDEs-Innovation-Economy.pdf.

4. Rise, created by Barclays, home page, accessed November 11, 2024, https://rise .barclays.

5. Oihana Basilio Ruiz de Apodaca, Fiona Murray, and Lars Frolund, "What Is 'Deep Tech' and What Are Deep Tech Ventures?" (working paper, MIT REAP, 2022), https://reap.mit.edu/assets/What_Is_Deep_Tech_MIT_2022.pdf.

6. "About NQCP," University of Copenhagen, https://nqcp.ku.dk/about-nqcp/.

7. Miriam Partington, "How Einstein's Old Stomping Ground Became Europe's Spinout Capital," Sifted, June 12, 2023, https://sifted.eu/articles/stanford-of-europe -spinouts.

8. Mercedes Delgado and Fiona E. Murray, "Mapping the Regions, Organizations, and Individuals That Drive Inclusion in the Innovation Economy," *Entrepreneurship and Innovation: Policy and Economy*, vol. 1 (Cambridge, MA: National Bureau of Economic Research, 2022).

9. Francesca McCaffrey, "A New Era in Fusion Research at MIT," MIT News, March 9, 2018, https://news.mit.edu/2018/new-era-fusion-research-mit-eni-0309.

10. More information on the fund at Engine Ventures (separate from its accelerator) can be found at https://engineventures.com.

11. "Team," Lakestar, accessed November 11, 2024, https://lakestar.com/team.

12. Sebastian Mallaby, *The Power Law: Venture Capital and the Making of the New Future* (New York: Penguin Press, 2022), 25. ARD used the term "risk capital" to differentiate its approach: "In recent months American Research has been erroneously compared to well-known, long-established investment companies. It should again be emphasized that American Research is a 'venture' or '*risk capital*' enterprise. The Corporation does not invest in the ordinary sense. It creates. It risks. Results take more time and the expenses of its operation must be higher, but the potential for ultimate profits is much greater" (italics added). See *ARD: Annual Reports (Bound), 1951–1956*. Georges F. Doriot papers, Mss:784 1921–1984 D698, Volume: 110. Baker Library Special Collections and Archives, Harvard Business School.

13. L. Rafael Reif, "A Better Way to Deliver Innovation to the World," *Washington Post*, May 22, 2015, https://www.washingtonpost.com/opinions/a-better-way-to-deliver-innovation-to-the-world/2015/05/22/35023680-fe28-11e4-8b6c-0dcce21e223d_story.html.

14. "About Us," Future Africa, accessed November 11, 2024, https://www.future.africa/about-us.

15. Katherine Boyle and David Ulevitch, "It's Time to Build for America: Announcing Our $500M Commitment to Companies Building in American Dynamism," Andreessen Horowitz, May 9, 2023, https://a16z.com/its-time-to-build-for-america-announcing-our-500m-commitment-to-companies-building-in-american-dynamism/.

16. Philip Budden and Fiona Murray, "Strategically Engaging with Innovation Ecosystems," *MIT Sloan Management Review*, Fall 2022, https://sloanreview.mit.edu/article/strategically-engaging-with-innovation-ecosystems/.

Chapter 4

1. Erin Griffith, "They Fled San Francisco. The AI Boom Pulled Them Back," *New York Times*, June 7, 2023, https://www.nytimes.com/2023/06/07/technology/ai-san-francisco-tech-industry.html.

2. Brandi Vincent, "Defense Innovation Unit Aims to Build upon Last Year's 'History-Making' Deliveries in 2023," DefenseScoop, January 25, 2023, https://defensescoop.com/2023/01/25/defense-innovation-unit-aims-to-build-upon-its-history-making-deliveries-in-2022/.

3. On lean start-up, business model canvas, and design thinking, see Steve Blank's *The Four Steps to the Epiphany: Successful Strategies for Products That Win* (Hoboken, NJ: John Wiley & Sons, 2003) and the rereleased version with the subtitle "The Book That Launched the Lean Startup Revolution" (Hoboken, NJ: John Wiley & Sons, 2020); Alexander Osterwalder and Yves Pigneur, *Business Model Generation: A Handbook for Visionaries, Game Changers, and Challengers* (Hoboken, NJ: John Wiley & Sons, 2010); Tim Brown, "Design Thinking," *Harvard Business Review*, June 2008, https://hbr.org/2008/06/design-thinking.

4. Luisa Zhou, "Startup Failure Statistics: What Percentage of Startups Fail?," blog, updated April 13, 2024, https://www.luisazhou.com/blog/startup-failure-statistics/.

5. Paul Graham, "How Y Combinator Started," March 2012, https://paulgraham.com/ycstart.html.

6. The Engine, home page, accessed November 11, 2024, https://engine.xyz; "NSF's Innovation Corps (I-Corps™)," US National Science Foundation, accessed November 11, 2024, https://new.nsf.gov/funding/initiatives/i-corps.

7. Noubar Afeyan and Gary P. Pisano, "What Evolution Can Teach Us about Innovation," *Harvard Business Review* 99, no. 5 (September–October 2021): 62–72, https://hbr.org/2021/09/what-evolution-can-teach-us-about-innovation.

8. Alison Wood Brooks, Laura Huang, Sarah Wood Kearney, and Fiona Murray, "Entrepreneurial Attraction: Investors Prefer Entrepreneurial Ventures Pitched by Attractive Men," *Proceedings of the National Academy of Science* 111, no. 12 (2014): 4427–4431.

9. Mercedes Delgado and Fiona E. Murray, "Faculty as Catalysts for Training New Inventors: Differential Outcomes for Male and Female PhD Students," *Proceedings of the National Academy of Sciences* 118, no. 45 (2021), https://doi.org/10.1073/pnas.2200684120.

10. Techstars, home page, accessed November 11, 2024, https://www.techstars.com.

11. Dava Sobel's highly readable account of the 1714 Longitude Prize, *Longitude: The True Story of a Lone Genius Who Solved the Greatest Scientific Problem of His Time* (London: Bloomsbury, 1995), also recounts some of the tragedies at sea that led a series of European governments to offer prizes for whomever could best provide a solution to determine longitude.

12. Lucas Spreiter, "Six Reasons Why T.U. Munich Keeps Winning the SpaceX Hyperloop Pod Competition and What This Taught Me about Innovation," Medium, December 14, 2018, https://medium.com/unetiq/six-reasons-why-tu-munich-keeps-winning-the-spacex-hyperloop-pod-competition-and-what-this-taught-c47aff9905dc.

13. "Intelligent Ship: Competition Document," GOV.UK, updated May 17, 2023, https://www.gov.uk/government/publications/intelligent-ship-phase-3-optimising

-for-the-human-in-a-human-autonomy-team-hat/the-intelligent-ship-competition
-document.

14. Alex Manson, "Nothing Ventured Nothing Gained," archived May 28, 2024, at
the Wayback Machine, https://web.archive.org/web/20240223004801/https://scven
tures.io/nothing-ventured-nothing-gained-the-scv-story/chapter-1/.

15. Daniel C. Fehder and Yael V. Hochberg, "Accelerators and the Regional Supply
of Venture Capital Investment" (working paper, Social Science Research Network,
2014), https://papers.ssrn.com/sol3/papers.cfm?abstract_id=2518668.

16. "BHP Xplor Selects Seven Companies to Help Accelerate Copper and Nickel
Exploration," BHP, January 17, 2023, https://www.bhp.com/news/articles/2023/01
/bhp-xplor-selects-seven-companies-to-help-accelerate-copper-and-nickel-exploration.

17. "Let's Work Together!," Startup Autobahn, accessed November 11, 2024, https://
startup-autobahn.com/partner/.

18. "Dubai Future Accelerators: Co-Creating the Future," Dubai Future Foundation,
accessed November 11, 2024, https://www.dubaifuture.ae/initiatives/future-design
-and-acceleration/dubai-future-accelerators.

19. M12, home page, accessed November 11, 2024, https://m12.vc.

Chapter 5

1. Deborah Ancona and Henrik Bresman, *X-Teams: How to Build Teams That Lead,
Innovate and Succeed* (Boston: Harvard Business Review Press, 2023). See also their
X-teams-related simulation, known as "xCHANGE" (online at https://www.xlead
.co), which gamifies innovation in a large organization.

2. The three levels of "nimble" leadership for innovation and entrepreneurship in a
large organization come from Deborah Ancona and Kate Isaacs (see, e.g., Meredith
Somers, "The 3 Leadership Types in a Nimble Organization," MIT Sloan, November
1, 2021, https://mitsloan.mit.edu/ideas-made-to-matter/3-leadership-types-a-nimble
-organization). They are also expanding their *Harvard Business Review* article,
"Nimble Leadership: Walking the Line between Creativity and Chaos" (July–August
2019, https://hbr.org/2019/07/nimble-leadership) into a book.

3. Elsbeth Johnson, *Step Up, Step Back: How to Really Deliver Strategic Change in Your
Organization* (London: Bloomsbury Business, 2020).

Chapter 6

1. The "three lenses" come from Deborah G. Ancona, Thomas A. Kochan, Maureen
Scully, John Van Maanen, and D. Eleanor Westney, *Managing for the Future: Organizational Behavior and Processes*, 3rd ed. (Stamford, CT: Thomson South-Western,

2004). We adopt and adapt this three lenses approach specifically for innovation; see Phil Budden and Fiona Murray, "Leading Innovation: Identifying Challenges and Opportunities Using MIT's Three Lenses" (working paper, MIT Lab for Innovation Science and Policy, 2020), https://reap.mit.edu/assets/Innovation-And-MITs-3-lenses.pdf.

2. A quote apparently made in a debate at a 2011 commencement address at the University of Carolina; see Bill Trott, "Obituary E. O. Wilson, Naturalist Dubbed a Modern-Day Darwin, Dies at 92," Reuters, December 27, 2021, https://www.reuters.com/lifestyle/science/obituary-modern-day-darwin-eo-wilson-dies-92-2021-12-27/.

3. Edgar H. Schein, *Organizational Culture and Leadership* (San Francisco: Jossey-Bass Publishers, 1992), https://doi.org/10.1177/027046769401400247.

4. Schein, *Organizational Culture and Leadership.*

5. Elsbeth Johnson and Fiona Murray. "What a Crisis Teaches Us about Innovation," *MIT Sloan Management Review*, Winter 2021, https://sloanreview.mit.edu/article/what-a-crisis-teaches-us-about-innovation/.

6. The full "Cultural Web" developed by Gerry Johnson and Kevan Scholes in 1992 is set out in their *Fundamentals of Strategy* book with Richard Whittington (Upper Saddle River, NJ: FT Press, 2011).

7. "The Skunk Works® Legacy," Lockheed Martin, accessed November 11, 2024, https://www.lockheedmartin.com/en-us/who-we-are/business-areas/aeronautics/skunkworks/skunk-works-origin-story.html.

8. E. O. Wilson, *Letters to a Young Scientist* (New York City: Liveright, 2013).

9. Innovation Leader (InnoLead), home page, accessed November 11, 2024, https://www.innovationleader.com.

Chapter 7

1. Enrico Moretti, *The New Geography of Job* (New York: HarperCollins, 2012).

2. Academic Centre of Excellence in Cyber Security Education, *The North West Cyber Corridor Innovation Impact Study: Evidence Base (2023)* (Lancaster, UK: Academic Centre of Excellence in Cyber Security Education, 2023), https://www.lancaster.ac.uk/media/lancaster-university/content-assets/images/security-lancaster/cyber-foundry/LancasterCyberCorridorImpactStudy.pdf.

3. Such as the UN Sustainable Development Goals, corporate social responsibility, and environmental, social, and governance criteria.

4. MIT Innovation Ecosystems, home page, accessed November 11, 2024, https://innovationecosystems.mit.edu.

5. MIT Sloan Executive Education, home page, accessed November 11, 2024, https://exec.mit.edu/s/; "MIT Executive MBA," MIT Sloan School of Management, November 11, 2024, https://mitsloan.mit.edu/emba/introduce-yourself.

6. "Corporate Innovation," MIT Management Executive Education, accessed November 11, 2024, https://corporateinnovation.mit.edu.

Acknowledgments

1. MIT REAP, home page, accessed November 11, 2024, https://reap.mit.edu.

Appendix

1. The on-demand "Accelerating Innovation through Ecosystems" sprint, from MIT Sloan Executive Education, is available online at https://exec.mit.edu/s/topic/corporate-innovation.

Selected Bibliography

Afeyan, Noubar, and Gary P. Pisano. "What Evolution Can Teach Us about Innovation." *Harvard Business Review* 99, no. 5 (September–October 2021): 62–72. https://hbr.org/2021/09/what-evolution-can-teach-us-about-innovation.

Ancona, Deborah, Thomas Kochan, Maureen Scully, John van Maanen, and Eleanor Westley. *Managing for the Future: Organizational Behavior and Processes.* Stamford, CT: Thomson South-Western, 2004.

Ancona, Deborah, and Henrik Bresman. *X-Teams: How to Build Teams That Lead, Innovate, and Succeed.* Boston: Harvard Business School Press, 2023.

Ancona, Deborah, Elaine Backman, and Kate Isaacs. "Nimble Leadership: Walking the Line between Creativity and Chaos." *Harvard Business Review* (July–August 2019): 74–83. https://hbr.org/2019/07/nimble-leadership.

Apodaca, Oihana Basilio Ruiz de, Fiona Murray, and Lars Frolund. "What Is 'Deep Tech' and What Are Deep Tech Ventures?" Working paper, MIT REAP, 2022. https://reap.mit.edu/assets/What_Is_Deep_Tech_MIT_2022.pdf.

"BHP Xplor Selects Seven Companies to Help Accelerate Copper and Nickel Exploration." BHP, January 17, 2023. Accessed November 11, 2024. https://www.bhp.com/news/articles/2023/01/bhp-xplor-selects-seven-companies-to-help-accelerate-copper-and-nickel-exploration.

Brooks, Alison Wood, Laura Huang, Sarah Wood Kearney, and Fiona Murray. "Entrepreneurial Attraction: Investors Prefer Entrepreneurial Ventures Pitched by Attractive Men." *Proceedings of the National Academy of Science* 111, no. 12 (2014): 4427–4431.

Brown, Tim. "Design Thinking." *Harvard Business Review*, June 2008. https://hbr.org/2008/06/design-thinking.

Budden, Phil, and Fiona Murray. "Leading Innovation: Identifying Challenges and Opportunities Using MIT's Three Lenses." Working paper, MIT Lab for Innovation

Science and Policy, 2020. https://reap.mit.edu/assets/Innovation-And-MITs-3-lenses .pdf.

Budden, Phil, and Fiona Murray. "MIT's Stakeholder Framework for Building and Accelerating Innovation Ecosystems." Working paper, MIT REAP, 2024. https://reap .mit.edu/assets/MIT-Stakeholder-Framework_Innovation-Ecosystems-23.pdf.

Budden, Phil, and Fiona Murray. "Strategically Engaging with Innovation Ecosystems." *MIT Sloan Management Review*, Fall 2022. https://sloanreview.mit.edu/article /strategically-engaging-with-innovation-ecosystems/.

Budden, Phil, Fiona Murray, Isaac Rahamim, Dylan Brown, and Nick Setterberg. "Kessel Run: An Innovation Opportunity for the US Air Force." Mission Innovation working paper, 2021 (now reposted on the Murray Lab website), https://murray-lab .org/wp-content/uploads/2024/08/Kessel-Run_compressed.pdf.

Budden, Phil, Fiona Murray, and Anna Turskaya. "A Systematic MIT Approach for Assessing 'Innovation-Driven Entrepreneurship' in Ecosystems." Working paper v.3.0, MIT REAP, 2024. https://reap.mit.edu/resource/assessing-the-system-and-capacities.

Budden, Phil, Fiona Murray, and Ogbogu Ukuku. "Differentiating Small Enterprises in the Innovation Economy: Start-Ups, New SMEs and Other Growth Ventures." Working paper, MIT Lab for Innovation Science and Policy, 2021. https://reap.mit .edu/assets/Differentiating-Small-Enterprises-IDEs-Innovation-Economy.pdf.

Cohen, David, and Brad Feld. *Do More Faster: Techstars Lessons to Accelerate your Startup*. Hoboken, NJ: John Wiley & Sons, Inc., 2010.

"Corporate Innovation." MIT Management Executive Education. Accessed November 11, 2024. https://corporateinnovation.mit.edu/.

DSM. Home page. Accessed November 11, 2024. https://www.dsm.com/corporate /home.html.

"Enduring Ideas: The Three Horizons of Growth." *McKinsey Quarterly*, December 1, 2009. https://www.mckinsey.com/capabilities/strategy-and-corporate-finance/our -insights/enduring-ideas-the-three-horizons-of-growth.

Engine, The. Home page. Accessed November 11, 2024. https://engine.xyz/.

Fairlie, Robert, and Sameeksha Desai. *National Report on Early-Stage Entrepreneurship in the United States: 2020*. Kansas City, MO: Ewing Marion Kauffman Foundation, 2021.

Fehder, Daniel C., and Yael V. Hochberg. "Accelerators and the Regional Supply of Venture Capital Investment." Working paper, Social Science Research Network, 2014. https://papers.ssrn.com/sol3/papers.cfm?abstract_id=2518668.

Feld, Brad, and Ian Hathaway. *The Startup Community Way: Evolving an Entrepreneurial Ecosystem*. Hoboken, NJ: John Wiley & Sons, Inc., 2020.

Gallucci, Maria, and Jeff St. John. "6 Innovative Startups That Are Kicking CO_2 Out of Cement and Concrete." Canary Media, October 24, 2023. https://www.canary media.com/articles/clean-industry/6-innovative-startups-that-are-kicking-co2-out-of -cement-and-concrete.

Gans, Joshua, Erin Scott, and Scott Stern. *Entrepreneurship: Choice and Strategy*. New York City: W. W. Norton & Co., 2025.

Gregersen, Hal, Clayton Christensen, and Jeff Dyer, "The Innovator's DNA," *Harvard Business Review*, December 2009. https://hbr.org/2009/12/the-innovators-dna.

Hall, Peter, and David Soskie. *Varieties of Capitalism: The Institutional Foundations of Comparative Advantage*. Oxford: Oxford University Press, 2001.

Hausman, Naomi. "University Innovation, Local Economic Growth, and Entrepreneurship." US Census Bureau Center for Economic Studies Paper No. CES-WP- 12-10, June 2012. https://papers.ssrn.com/sol3/papers.cfm?abstract_id=2097842.

"Held in High Regard—Nova Scotia Is Home to the Highest Concentration of Ocean Scientists in the World." Pro-Oceanus, November 20, 2012. https://pro-oceanus.com /about/news?c=held-in-high-regard-nova-scotia-is-home-to-the-highest-concentration -of-ocean-scientists-in-the-world.

Innovation Leader. Home page. Accessed November 11, 2024, https://www.innova tionleader.com.

"Intelligent Ship: Competition Document." GOV.UK, updated May 17, 2023. https://www.gov.uk/government/publications/intelligent-ship-phase-3-optimising -for-the-human-in-a-human-autonomy-team-hat/the-intelligent-ship-competition -document.

Johnson, Elsbeth. *Step Up, Step Back: How to Really Deliver Strategic Change in Your Organization*. London: Bloomsbury Business, 2020.

Johnson, Elsbeth, and Fiona Murray. "What a Crisis Teaches Us about Innovation." *MIT Sloan Management Review*, Winter 2021. https://sloanreview.mit.edu/article/what -a-crisis-teaches-us-about-innovation/.

Johnson, Gerry, Richard Whittington, and Kevan Scholes. *Fundamentals of Strategy*. 2nd ed. Upper Saddle River, NJ: FT Press, 2011.

M12. Home page. Accessed November 11, 2024. https://m12.vc/.

Malone, Scott. "GE's Immelt Hopes Move to Boston Fuels Staff 'Paranoia.'" Reuters, March 2016. https://www.reuters.com/article/ge-headquarters-idINL2N16W12L.

Manning, Catherine G. "Technology Readiness Levels." NASA, September 27, 2023. https://www.nasa.gov/directorates/somd/space-communications-navigation-program /technology-readiness-levels/.

Miano, Tim, and Fiona Murray. "Innovation Systems: Blueprints and Lessons from MIT." 2024. https://www.innovation-blueprints.com.

"MIT Executive MBA." MIT Sloan School of Management. Accessed November 11, 2024. https://mitsloan.mit.edu/emba/introduce-yourself.

MIT Innovation Ecosystems. Home page. Accessed November 11, 2024. https://innovationecosystems.mit.edu.

"MIT.nano Announces Founding Members of Its Corporate Consortium." MIT News. Accessed November 11, 2024. https://news.mit.edu/2019/mit-nano-announces-corporate-consortium-founding-members-0708.

MIT REAP. Home page. Accessed November 11, 2024. https://reap.mit.edu/.

MIT Sloan Executive Education. Home page. Accessed November 11, 2024. https://exec.mit.edu/s/.

Mokyr, Joel. *The Enlightened Economy: An Economic History of Britain 1700–1850*. New Haven, CT: Yale University Press, 2009.

Mokyr, Joel. "Entrepreneurship and the Industrial Revolution in Britain." In *The Invention of Enterprise: Entrepreneurship from Ancient Mesopotamia to Modern Times*, edited by David S. Landes, Joel Mokyr, and William Baumol, 183–210. Princeton, NJ: Princeton University Press, 2012.

Moretti, Enrico. *New Geography of Jobs*. New York: HarperCollins, 2012.

"NSF's Innovation Corps (I-Corps™)." NSF. Accessed November 11, 2024. https://new.nsf.gov/funding/initiatives/i-corps.

Osterwalder, Alexander, and Yves Pigneur. *Business Model Generation: A Handbook for Visionaries, Game Changers, and Challengers*. Hoboken, NJ: Wiley, 2010.

Raff, Stefan, Fiona E. Murray, and Martin Murmann. "Why You Should Tap Innovation at Deep-Tech Startups." *MIT Sloan Management Review*, August 26, 2024. https://sloanreview.mit.edu/article/why-you-should-tap-innovation-at-deep-tech-startups/.

Repenning, Nelson, Don Kieffer, and Todd Astor. "The Most Underrated Skill in Management." *MIT Sloan Management Review*, Spring 2017. https://sloanreview.mit.edu/article/the-most-underrated-skill-in-management/.

Repenning, Nelson, and John Sterman. "Nobody Ever Gets Credit for Fixing Problems That Never Happened: Creating and Sustaining Process Improvement." *California Management Review* 43, no. 5 (Summer 2001): 64–88.

Rise, created by Barclays. Home page. Accessed November 11, 2024. https://rise.barclays/.

Rothwell, Jonathan, José Lobo, Deborah Strumsky, and Mark Muro. "Patenting and Innovation in Metropolitan America." Brookings, February 1, 2013. https://www.brookings.edu/articles/patenting-and-innovation-in-metropolitan-america/.

Shah, Raj and Christopher Kirchoff. *Unit X: How the Pentagon and Silicon Valley Are Transforming the Future of War.* New York City: Simon & Schuster, 2024.

Small, Andrew. "Why GE Moved to Boston, According to Its CEO." Bloomberg.com, September 29, 2016. https://www.bloomberg.com/news/articles/2016-09-29/why-general-electric-moved-to-boston.

Somers, Meredith. "The 3 Leadership Types in a Nimble Organization." MIT Sloan, November 1, 2021. https://mitsloan.mit.edu/ideas-made-to-matter/3-leadership-types-a-nimble-organization.

Spreiter, Lucas. "Six Reasons Why TU Munich Keeps Winning the SpaceX Hyperloop Pod Competition and What This Taught Me about Innovation." Medium, December 14, 2018. https://medium.com/unetiq/six-reasons-why-tu-munich-keeps-winning-the-spacex-hyperloop-pod-competition-and-what-this-taught-c47aff9905dc.

"Taking Mining Technology into Orbit." CSIRO, April 18, 2023. https://www.csiro.au/en/news/All/Articles/2023/April/Taking-mining-technology-into-orbit.

Techstars Global Startup Network. Home page. Accessed November 11, 2024. https://www.techstars.com/.

Trott, Bill. "Obituary E. O. Wilson, Naturalist Dubbed a Modern-Day Darwin, Dies at 92." Reuters, December 27, 2021. https://www.reuters.com/lifestyle/science/obituary-modern-day-darwin-eo-wilson-dies-92-2021-12-27/.

United States Congress House Committee on Science and Technology. Subcommittee on Space Science and Applications. *NASA Program Management and Procurement Procedures and Practices: Hearings before the Subcommittee on Space Science and Applications of the Committee on Science and Technology, US House of Representatives, Ninety-Seventh Congress, First Session, June 24, 25, 1981.* Washington, DC: US Government Printing Office, 1981.

Vincent, Brandi. "Defense Innovation Unit Aims to Build upon Last Year's 'History-Making' Deliveries in 2023." DefenseScoop, January 25, 2023. https://defensescoop.com/2023/01/25/defense-innovation-unit-aims-to-build-upon-its-history-making-deliveries-in-2022/.

"Working-from-Home Illusion Fades, The." *The Economist*, June 28, 2023. https://www.economist.com/finance-and-economics/2023/06/28/the-working-from-home-delusion-fades.

Index

Page numbers in italics refer to figures.